Routledge Revivals

The Methuen Book of Shakespeare Anecdotes

Few playwrights have been more slandered, abused or honoured in performance than William Shakespeare.

First published in 1992, this collection of 300 stories focuses on Shakespeare's plays on stage. Organised chronologically, it offers the reader the opportunity to witness the changes in theatrical approaches to Shakespeare from their own time to the present day.

This book will be of interest to those studying theatre, but also to those fascinated by the Shakespeare tradition.

The Methuen Book of Shakespeare Anecdotes

Compiled and Edited by
Ralph Berry

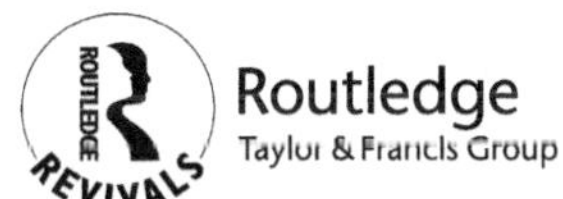

First published in 1992
by Methuen Drama

This edition first published in 2016 by Routledge
2 Park Square, Milton Park, Abingdon, Oxon, OX14 4RN
and by Routledge
711 Third Avenue, New York, NY 10017

Routledge is an imprint of the Taylor & Francis Group, an informa business

Publisher's Note
The publisher has gone to great lengths to ensure the quality of this reprint but points out that some imperfections in the original copies may be apparent.

Disclaimer
The publisher has made every effort to trace copyright holders and welcomes correspondence from those they have been unable to contact.

ISBN 13: 978-1-138-65956-8 (hbk)

ISBN 13: 978-1-315-62010-7 (ebk)
ISBN 13: 978-1-138-65959-9 (pbk)

The Methuen Book of

SHAKESPEARE ANECDOTES

COMPILED AND EDITED BY

Ralph Berry

Methuen Drama

First published in Great Britain in 1992
by Methuen Drama,
Michelin House, 81 Fulham Road, London SW3 6RB

A CIP catalogue record for this book
is available from the British Library

ISBN 0 413 66500 3

The illustration on the front jacket shows Edmund Kean as Richard III with John Cooper as Richmond in *Richard III.* It is reproduced by courtesy of the Board of Trustees of the Victoria & Albert Museum.

Printed in Great Britain
by Clays Ltd, St Ives plc

Contents

Acknowledgements

For permission to reproduce the extracts in this collection, grateful acknowledgement is made to the following:

For William W. Appleton's *Charles Macklin* (Harvard University Press, 1960), © 1960 William W. Appleton, to the publishers; for Kathleen Barker's *The Theatre Royal Bristol 1766–1966* (1974), © 1974 Kathleen Barker, to the Society for Theatre Research; for Sally Beauman's *The Royal Shakespeare Company: A History of Ten Decades* (Oxford University Press, 1982), © 1982 Sally Beauman, to Peters Fraser & Dunlop Ltd; for Elizabeth Belsey's letter to *The Times* (17 August 1988), © 1988 Elizabeth Belsey, to the author; for Jean Benedetti's *Stanislavski: A Biography* (Methuen, 1988), © 1988 Jean Benedetti, to the Octopus Publishing Group; for Claire Bloom's *Limelight and After* (Weidenfeld and Nicolson, 1982), © 1982 Claire Bloom, to the publishers; for Melvyn Bragg's *RICH: The Life of Richard Burton* (Hodder & Stoughton, 1988), © 1988 Melvyn Bragg Ltd and Sally Burton (in the notebooks, journals and letters of Richard Burton © 1987 Sally Burton), to the publishers and Richard Scott Simon Ltd; for Kenneth Branagh's *Beginning* (Chatto & Windus, 1989), © 1989 Kenneth Branagh, to Random Century Group; for Edward Braun's *The Director and the Stage* (Methuen, 1982), © 1982 Edward Braun, to the Octopus Publishing Group; for 'Briefing' (*The Times*, 9 August 1990), © 1990 *The Times*, to *The Times*; for Philip Brockbanks's *Players of Shakespeare* (Cambridge University Press, 1985), © 1985 Philip Brockbank, to the publishers; for Simon Callow's *Being an Actor* (Methuen, 1984), © 1984 Simon Callow, to the Octopus Publishing Group; for Simon Callow's *Charles Laughton: A Difficult Actor* (Methuen, 1987), © 1987 Simon Callow, to the Octopus Publishing Group and Grove Weidenfeld; for Humphrey Carpenter's *OUDS: A Centenary History of the Oxford University Dramatic Society 1885–1985* (Oxford University Press, 1985), © 1985 Humphrey Carpenter, to the publishers; for Kathryn Cave's *The Diary of Joseph Farington*, Volume XI, (Yale University Press, 1983), © 1983 Kathryn Cave, to the publishers; for L.W. Connolly's *The Censorship of English Drama 1737–1824* (1976), © 1976 L.W. Connolly, to the Henry E. Huntington Library; for Richard David's *Shakespeare in the Theatre* (Cambridge University Press, 1978), © 1978 Richard David, to the publishers; for Basil Dean's *Seven Ages* (Hutchinson, 1970), © 1970 Basil Dean, to Martin Dean on behalf of the Estate of Basil Dean; for 'Diary' (*The Times*, 26 June 1991), © 1991 *The Times*, to *The Times*; for Brian

Dobbs's *Drury Lane: Three Centuries of the Theatre Royal 1663–1971* (Cassell, 1972), © 1972 Brian Dobbs, to Macmillan Publishing Company; for Richard Eyre's 'The Hamlyn Lecture' (July, 1991), © 1991 Richard Eyre, to Richard Eyre; for Herbert Farjeon's *The Shakespearean Scene: Dramatic Criticisms* (Hutchinson, 1949), © 1949 Herbert Farjeon, to David Higham Associates; for Attilio Favorini's 'Richard's Himself Again' (*Educational Theatre Journal*, 1972, 403–414) © 1972 Attilio Favorini, to the Johns Hopkins University Press; for Felix Felton's 'Max Reinhardt in England' (*Theatre Research/Récherches Théâtrales*, 1963), © 1963 Felix Felton, to the publishers; for Bryan Forbes's *That Despicable Race: A History of the British Acting Tradition* (Hamish Hamilton, 1980), © 1980 Bryan Forbes, to the publishers; for Richard Foulkes's *Shakespeare and the Victorian Stage* (Cambridge University Press, 1986), © 1986 Richard Foulkes, to the publishers; for Gene Fowler's *Good Night, Sweet Prince (The Life and Times of John Barrymore)*, © 1943 and 1944 Gene Fowler, renewed 1970 and 1971 by A. Fowler, G. Fowler, Jr., J.F. Morrison and W. Fowler, to the heirs of Gene Fowler; for Sean French's 'Diary' (*New Statesman and Nation*, 23 March 1989), © 1989 Sean French, to the *Observer*; for William Gaskill's *A Sense of Direction* (Faber & Faber, 1988), © 1988 William Gaskill, to the publishers; for Maurice Good's *Every Inch A Lear* (Sono Nis Press, Victoria, Canada, 1982), © 1982 Maurice Good, to the publishers; for John Goodwin's *Peter Hall's Diaries* (Hamish Hamilton, 1983), © 1983 John Goodwin, to Hamish Hamilton and Harper Collins Publishers; for Tyrone Guthrie's *A Life in the Theatre* (Hamish Hamilton, 1960), © 1960 Tyrone Guthrie, to the publishers; for Julie Hankey's *Richard III* (Plays in Performance series, Bristol Classic Press, 1981), © 1981 Julie Hankey, to the publishers; for Ronald Harwood's *The Ages of Gielgud: An Actor at Eighty* (Hodder & Stoughton, 1984), © 1984 Ronald Harwood, to the publishers; for Ronald Harwood's *Sir Donald Wolfit C.B.E.: his life and work in the unfashionable theatre* (1971), © 1971 Ronald Harwood, to Sheil Land Associates Ltd; for Charles Beecher Hogan's *Shakespeare in the Theatre 1701–1800* (Oxford University Press, 1952), © 1952 Charles Beecher Hogan, to the publishers; for John Houseman's *Unfinished Business* (Chatto and Windus, 1986), © 1986 John Houseman, to Random Century Group; for Dennis Kennedy's *Granville Barker and the Dream of Theatre* (Cambridge University Press, 1985), © 1985 Dennis Kennedy, to the publishers; for John Lahr's *The Orton Diaries* (Methuen, 1986), © 1986 the Estate of Joe Orton, deceased, to the Octopus Publishing Group and Margaret Ramsay Ltd; for Osbert Lancaster's *With an Eye to the Future* (Hutchinson, 1986), © 1986 Osbert Lancaster, to John Murray (Publishers) Ltd; for Matheson Lang's *Mr Wu Looks Back* (Stanley Paul, 1941), © 1941 Matheson Lang, to Random Century Group; for John Lawlor and W.H. Auden's *To Nevill Coghill From Friends* (Faber & Faber, 1966), © 1966 John Lawlor and W.H. Auden, to the publishers; for Barbara Leaming's *Orson Welles: A Biography* (Weidenfeld and Nicolson, 1985), © 1985 Barbara Leaming, to the publishers and to Sheil Land Associates; for David M. Little and George M. Kahrl's *The Letters of David Garrick* (Harvard University Press, 1963), © 1963 David M. Little and George M.

Kahrl, to the publishers; for Margaret McCall's *My Drama School* (Robson Books, 1978), © 1978 Margaret McCall, to the publishers; for W. Macqueen Pope's *The Curtain Rises* (1961), © 1961 W. Macqueen Pope, to Thomas Nelson and Sons Ltd; for W. Macqueen Pope's *Carriages at Eleven* (1947), © 1947 W. Macqueen Pope, *Ghosts and Greasepaint* (1951), © 1951 W. Macqueen Pope and *St James's Theatre of Distinction* (1958), © 1958 W. Macqueen Pope, to Rupert Crew Ltd on behalf of the Estate of W. Macqueen Pope; for Ian McKellen's contribution to *For Ian Charleson: A Tribute* (Constable, 1990), introduction © 1990 Ewen MacLaughlan, to Constable Publishers and Ian McKellen; for Leslie A. Marchand's *Byron's Letters and Journals* (1973), © 1973 Leslie A. Marchand, to John Murray (Publishers) Ltd and Harvard University Press; for Yvonne Mitchell's *Actress* (Routledge, 1957), © 1957 Yvonne Mitchell, to the publishers; for Mary Nash's *The Provoked Wife: The Life and Times of Susannah Cibber* (Hutchinson, 1977), © 1977 Mary Nash, to Random Century Group; for Neped L. Nelson and Gilbert B. Cross's *Drury Lane Journal: Selections from James Winston's Diaries 1819–1827* (1974), © 1974 Neped L. Nelson and Gilbert B. Cross, to the Society for Theatre Research; for Cathleen Nesbitt's *A Little Love and Good Company* (Faber & Faber, 1975), © 1975 Cathleen Nesbitt, to Faber & Faber and Stemmer House Publishers USA; for Gary O'Connor's *Ralph Richardson: An Actor's Life* (Hodder & Stoughton, 1982), © 1982 Gary O'Connor, to the publishers; for Laurence Olivier's *Confessions of an Actor* (Weidenfeld and Nicolson, 1982), © 1982 Laurence Olivier, to the publishers; for Laurence Olivier's *On Acting* (Sceptre, 1986), © 1986 Laurence Olivier, to Hodder & Stoughton Ltd; for Hesketh Pearson's *Modern Men and Mummers* (1974), © 1974 Hesketh Pearson, to A.P. Watt Ltd on behalf of Michael Holroyd; for Joseph G. Price's *The Triple Bond* (University Park: The Pennsylvania State University Press, 1975), © 1975 The Pennsylvania State University, to the publishers; for Clive Priestly's *Financial Scrutiny of the Royal Shakespeare Company* (London: HMSO, 1984), © 1984 HMSO, to Her Majesty's Stationery Office; for John Ripley's *'Julius Caesar' on Stage in England and America* (Cambridge University Press, 1980), © 1980 John Ripley, to the publishers; for Marvin Rosenberg's *The Masks of Othello* (1961), © 1961 Marvin Rosenberg, to the author; for Alfred Rossi's *Astonish Us in the Morning: Tyrone Guthrie Remembered* (1980), © 1980 Alfred Rossi, to the Random Century Group; for David Selbourne's *The Making of A Midsummer Night's Dream* (1982), © 1982 David Selbourne, to the author; for George Bernard Shaw's letters to William Archer, 16 March 1885 and to Alan S. Downer, 21 January 1948, to the Society of Authors on behalf of the Bernard Shaw Estate; for George Bernard Shaw's 'From the Point of View of a Playwright', to the Society of Authors on behalf of the Bernard Shaw Estate; for Antony Sher's *Year of the King* (Chatto & Windus, 1985), © 1985 Antony Sher, to Antony Sher; for Nicholas Shrimpton's 'Shakespeare Performances in Stratford-upon-Avon and London, 1982–3' (*Shakespeare Survey*, 37, 1984), © 1984 Nicholas Shrimpton, to Cambridge University Press; for Simone Signoret's *Nostalgia Ain't What It Used To Be* (Weidenfeld and Nicolson, 1978), © 1978 Simone Signoret, to the publishers; for Edith Sitwell's *English Eccentrics* (Faber & Faber, 1957), © 1957 Edith Sitwell, to David Higham Associates; for Robert Speaight's *William Poel and the Elizabethan Revival* (Heinemann, 1954), © 1954 Robert Speaight, to the Octopus Publishing Group; for Clive Swift's *The Job of Acting* (W. H. Allen, 1984), © 1984 Clive Swift, to Virgin Publishing; for J.C. Trewin's *Alec Clunes* (Barrie and Jenkins, 1958), © 1958 J.C. Trewin, to Random Century Group; for J.C. Trewin's *Benson and the Bensonians* (Hutchinson, 1960), © 1960 J.C. Trewin, to Random Century Group; for J.C. Trewin's *The Birmingham Repertory Theatre 1913–1963* (Barrie and Jenkins, 1963), © 1963 J.C. Trewin, to Random Century Group; for J.C. Trewin's *Shakespeare on the English Stage 1900–1964* (Barrie and Jenkins, 1964), © 1964 J.C. Trewin, to Random Century Group; for J.C. Trewin's *Sybil Thorndike* (Eyre & Spottiswoode, 1955), © 1955 J.C. Trewin, to Methuen London incorporating Eyre & Spottiswoode; for Kathleen Tynan's *The Life of Kenneth Tynan* (Weidenfeld and Nicolson, 1987), © 1987 Kathleen Tynan, to the publishers; for Irene Vanbrugh's *To Tell My Story* (Hutchinson, 1948), © 1948 Irene Vanbrugh, to Random Century Group; and for J. Michael Walton's *Craig on Theatre* (Methuen, 1983), © 1983 J. Michael Walton, to the Octopus Publishing Group.

The editor and publisher have taken all possible care to trace the copyright of all extracts reprinted in this volume, and to make acknowledgement of their use. If any errors have accidentally occurred, they will be corrected in subsequent editions, provided notification is sent to the publisher.

Introduction

Shakespeare on stage is this book's territory. I have sought to put together a collection of anecdotes, broadly in chronological order, that move from Shakespeare's day to our own. The result is four centuries of Shakespeariana, a kind of alternative history of the stage.

Every anthologist finds himself expounding his principles, and then explaining why their original purity has had to be diluted. 'Anecdote' comes first. A strict definition will not do: the element of intention is absent from many of the pieces here. An eighteenth-century writer will often introduce a story with some such phrase as 'I will now relate an Anecdote concerning Mr . . .' He believes the story to be, as the *OED* puts it, 'in itself interesting or striking'. He presents it in that belief. But certain passages here are not 'presented' by the author at all. They contain emergent facts, which we may find interesting, like the virtual censorship of *King Lear* during the latter years of the mad King George III. Again, take Pepys. He is not writing anecdotes, but recording a day's events in his diary. Still, the concentration of his entries, especially when focused on an evening in the playhouse, gives them a crisp anecdotal quality. One would be insane to reject Pepys on a formula. 'Anecdote', then, comes in on a broad gauge. I find each passage interesting and hope that my readers will agree.

Then, Shakespeare. This collection is concerned only with the stage dimension of Shakespeare, and the purely literary aspects are excluded. This can be vexatious. I should have liked to include, say, the eighteenth-century Librarian of the Bodleian who disposed of its copy of the First Folio to make way for the 'superior' Third Folio. It was many years before the Bodleian got its First Folio back. But no exercise of casuistry could justify the anecdote, which belongs to a history of literary values and taste. All the anecdotes here are concerned with or associated with the performance of Shakespeare's plays.

Location is also a question to be settled. The great bulk of these anecdotes are from the English stage. But the American stage is also here, beginning with the performance of *Othello* for the Cherokees in Williamsburg, Virginia, in 1752. And I could not resist the performances of *Hamlet* on board Captain William Keeling's ship in 1607. One would have liked a clear-cut principle of inclusion; but the stage defies consistency, and so does Shakespeare.

My coverage here is subject to certain unavoidable pressures. It is not possible to make a radically different selection for the seventeenth century. The range of available anecdotes is known, and cannot significantly be added to. Things begin to improve in the eighteenth century, with a much wider variety of materials; and the anthologist comes into his own in the nineteenth century. In the twentieth century one has free play, because the twentieth century is still going on; and one can make the modest but truthful claim that there is material here never anthologised before. A balance has to be struck between old and new. There is no virtue in excluding a favourite anecdote of Garrick, simply because it is well known. But even in the more remote eras (where the supply of material is very limited) I hope that my readers will find that some, at least, of these anecdotes are new to them. And they can be assured of some unfamiliar matter in the later stages of this collection.

The basic substance of this book is, of course, actors' stories. It was always so and always will be. Stage stories tend to be about, and related by, actors. I daresay that many readers will turn first to the reminiscences of their favourite actors. But in the twentieth century comes the rise of another figure, the director; and I have made a continuing effort to see that directors and their methods are well represented here. William Poel, Theodore Komisarjevsky, Tyrone Guthrie,

Peter Brook, above all the great Harley Granville-Barker: all of these have shaped the Shakespeare that we see on stage today. It is fitting for them to be memorialised in a collection that takes as its inspiration Shakespeare.

He comes to us through a multitude of episodes: affrays and riots, royal connections, astounding first-night triumphs, poignant leave-takings, accidents and recoveries, the minutiae of the actor's trade, smart ripostes and awesome blunders, curiosa of all kinds. Of Shakespeare as an actor, we have only the tradition that he played the Ghost in *Hamlet* and Adam in *As You Like It.* Of his successors, we have all manner of tales, and the selection I offer here is a homage to the richness and complexity of the Shakespearian tradition. In the end, what one glimpses through these episodes is not a simulacrum of life, but the thing itself.

William Shakespeare

Actor and playwright, 1564–1616

His Name is Printed, as the Custom was in those Times, amongst those of the other Players, before some old Plays, but without any particular Account of what sort of Parts he us'd to play; and tho' I have inquir'd, I could never meet with any further Account of him this way, than that the top of his Performance was the Ghost in his own *Hamlet*.

Nicholas Rowe, 'Some Account of the life, &c. of Mr William Shakespear', in Shakespeare, *Works*, ed. Rowe, 1709, I, ix.

Shakespeare seems also to have played Adam in *As You Like It*.

. . . this opportunity made them [the actors] greedily inquisitive into every little circumstance, more especially in his dramatick character, which his brother could relate of him. But he, it seems, was so stricken in years, and possibly his memory so weakened with infirmities (which might make him the easier pass for a man of weak intellects) that he could give them but little light into their enquiries; and all that could be recollected from him of his brother *Will*, in that station was, the faint, general, and almost lost idea he had of having once seen him act a part in one of his own comedies, wherein being to personate a decrepit old man, he wore a long beard, and appeared so weak and drooping and unable to walk, that he was forced to be supported and carried by another person to a table, at which he was seated among some company, who were eating, and one of them sung a song.

Shakespeare, *Plays*, ed. Samuel Johnson and George Steevens, 1778, I, 204.

His Aquaintance with *Ben Johnson* began with a remarkable piece of Humanity and good Nature; Mr. *Johnson*, who was at that Time altogether unknown to the World, had offer'd one of his Plays to the Players, in order to have it acted; and the Persons into whose Hands it was put, after having turn'd it carelessly and superciliously over, were just upon returning it to him with an ill-natur'd Answer, that it would be of no service to their Company, when *Shakespear* luckily cast his Eye upon it, and found something so well in it as to engage him first to read it through, and afterwards to recommend Mr. *Johnson* and his Writings to the Publick. After this they were profess'd Friends; tho' I don't know whether the other ever made him an equal return of Gentleness and Sincerity.

Nicholas Rowe, 'Some Account of the Life, &c. of Mr William Shakespear', in Shakespeare, *Works*, ed. Rowe, 1709, I, xii–xiii.

I remember, the players have often mentioned it as an honour to Shakespeare, that in his writing (whatsoever he penned) he never blotted out line. My answer hath been, would he had blotted a thousand. Which they thought a malevolent speech. I had not told posterity this, but for their ignorance, who choose that circumstance to commend their friend by, wherein he most faulted, and to justify mine own candour, for I loved the man, and do honour his memory (on this side idolatry) as much as any. He was indeed honest, and of an open, and free nature; had an excellent phantasy, brave notions, and gentle expressions, wherein he flowed with that facility, that sometimes it was necessary he should be stopped: *Sufflaminandus erat*, as Augustus said of Haterius. His wit was in his own power; would the rule of it had been so too. Many times he fell into those things, could not escape laughter, as when he said in the person of Caesar, one speaking to him, 'Caesar thou dost me wrong' – he replied: 'Caesar did never wrong, but with just cause,' and such like, which were ridiculous.* But he redeemed his vices, with his virtues. There was ever more in him to be praised, than to be pardoned.

Ben Jonson, *Timber: or, Discoveries; Made upon Men and Matter*, 1641, in Ben Jonson, *Workes*, pp. 97–8.

•

A Swiss traveller sees an early performance of *Julius Caesar*.

After dinner on the 21st of September [1599], at about two o'clock, I went with my companions over the water, and in the strewn roof-house saw the tragedy of the first Emperor Julius with at least fifteen characters very well acted. At the end of the comedy they danced according to their custom with extreme elegance. Two in men's clothes and two in women's gave this performance, in wonderful combination with each other.

Thomas Platter, from *Travels in England*, 1599; E.K. Chambers, *The Elizabethan Stage*, 1923, II, 365.

*These words do not appear in *Julius Caesar*. Instead occurs 'Know, Caesar doth not wrong; nor without cause/Will he be satisfied' (III.i.47–8). A reasonable inference is that Shakespeare revised the passage in response to criticism. But in 1972, Trevor Nunn restored Shakespeare's first thoughts, in his RSC production. And the line worked well, as a self-conscious paradox of Caesar's.

The tradition that *The Merry Wives of Windsor* was personally commissioned by Queen Elizabeth I was first mentioned by John Dennis, critic and playwright, 1657–1734, in the prefatory epistle to his adaptation of that play.

That this Comedy was not despicable, I guess'd for several Reasons: First, I knew very well, that it had pleas'd one of the greatest Queens that ever was in the World . . . This Comedy was written at her Command, and by her direction, and she was so eager to see it Acted, that she commanded it to be finished in fourteen days; and was afterwards, as Tradition tells us, very well pleas'd at the Representation.

John Dennis, The Epistle Dedicatory,
The Comical Gallant: or The Amours of Sir John Falstaffe, 1702.

Richard II was in its early years a dangerously political play, because it concerns the deposition of a reigning monarch. Shortly before the abortive coup d'état of the Earl of Essex in February 1601, his followers induced the Chamberlain's men to put on an extra performance of *Richard II.* The idea was to predispose the populace to the conspirators' cause, by proposing an analogue to the Queen. Following the collapse of the coup, the authorities examined Augustine Phillips of the Chamberlain's men.

The Examination of Augustine Phillips, servant unto the L. Chamberlain and one of his players, taken the xviijth of February, 1600, upon his oath.

'He saith that on Friday last was sennight or Thursday Sir Charles Percy Sir Josceline Percy and the Lord Mounteagle with some three more spoke to some of the players in the presence of this Examinate to have the play of the deposing and killing of King Richard the Second to be played the Saturday next, promising to get them xl*s*. more than their ordinary to play it. Where this Examinate and his fellows were determined to have played some other play, holding that play of King Richard to be so old and so long out of use that they should have small or no company at it. But at their request this Examinate and his fellows were content to play it the Saturday and had their xl*s* more than their ordinary for it, and so played it accordingly.'

E.K. Chambers, *The Elizabethan Stage*, 1923, II, 205.

Later in 1601, Queen Elizabeth gave her views on the playing of *Richard II* to William Lambarde, the antiquary. Lambarde made a memorandum of the meeting.

That which passed from the Excellent Majestie of Queen ELIZABETH *in her Privie Chamber at East Greenwich*, 4° *Augusti* 1601, 43° *Req. sui, towards* WILLIAM LAMBARDE.

He presented her Majestie with his Pandecta of all her rolls, bundells, membranes, and parcells that he reposed in her Majestie's Tower at London; whereof she had given to him the charge 21st January last past . . . she proceeded to further pages, and asked where she found cause of stay . . . so her Majestie fell upon the reign of King Richard II, saying 'I am Richard II. Know ye not that?'

W.L. 'Such a wicked imagination was determined and attempted by a most unkind Gent. the most adorned creature that ever your Majestie made.'

Her Majestie. 'He that will forget God, will also forget his benefactors; this tragedy was played 40^{tie} times in open streets and houses.'

The Shakespere Allusion-Book: A Collection of Allusions to Shakespere, from 1591 to 1700, ed. John Munro, 1909, I, 100.

From Captain William Keeling's journal of a voyage to the East Indies.

1607, Sept. 5. I sent the interpreter, according to his desier, abord the Hector whear he brooke fast, and after came abord mee, wher we gave the tragedie of Hamlett.

30. Captain Hawkins dined with me, wher my companions acted Kinge Richard the Second.

1608, Mar. 31. I envited Captain Hawkins to a ffishe dinner, and had Hamlet acted abord me: which I permitt to keepe my people from idlenes and unlawful games, or sleepe.

The Shakespeare Allusion-Book, 1909, I, x.

. . . I will entertain you at the present with what has happened this week at the Bank's side. The King's players had a new play, called *All is True*, representing some principal pieces of the reign of Henry VIII, which was set forth with many extraordinary circumstances of pomp and majesty, even to the matting of the stage; the Knights of the Order with their Georges and garters, the Guards with their embroidered coats, and the like: sufficient in truth within a while to make greatness very familiar, if not ridiculous. Now, King Henry making a masque at the Cardinal Wolsey's house, and certain chambers being shot off at his entry, some of the paper, or other stuff, wherewith one of them was stopped, did light on the thatch, where being thought at first but an idle smoke, and their eyes more attentive to the show, it kindled inwardly, and ran around like a train, consuming within less than an hour the whole house to the very grounds. This was the fatal period of that virtuous fabric, wherein yet nothing did perish but wood and straw, and a few forsaken cloaks; only one man had his breeches set on fire, that would perhaps have broiled him, if he had not by the benefit of a provident wit put it out with bottle ale.

Sir Henry Wotton to Sir Edmund Bacon,
2 July 1613; Logan Pearsall Smith,
Letters of Wotton, 1907, II, 32.

James I's favourite, the Duke of Buckingham, contemplates an earlier holder of his title. The Duke did not live out the month of this performance, being assassinated on 23 August.

On Tuesday his Grace [the Duke of Buckingham] was present at the acting of King Henry VIII at the Globe, a play bespoken of purpose by himself: whereat he stayed till the Duke of Buckingham was beheaded, then departed. Some say, he should rather have seen the fall of Cardinal Wolsey, who was a more lively type of himself, having governed this kingdom eighteen years, as he has done fourteen.

Robert Gell, *Letter to Sir Martyn Stuteville*, dated 9 August 1628. Printed in the Shakespeare Society's *Papers*, 1845, II, 151.

Romeo and Juliet at Lincoln's Inn Fields, 1662.

Note, There being a Fight and Scuffle in this Play, between the House of *Capulet*, and House of *Paris [sic]*; Mrs. *Holden* Acting his Wife, enter'd in a Hurry, Crying, O my Dear *Count*! She Inadvertently left out, O, in the pronuntiation of the Word *Count*! giving it a Vehement Accent, put the House into such a Laughter, that *London* Bridge at low-water was silence to it.

John Downes, *Roscius Anglicanus, Or An Historical Review of the Stage*, 1708, p. 22.

Samuel Pepys

Diarist, 1633–1703

6 January 1663

So to my brother's, where Creed and I and my wife dined with Tom, and after dinner to the Duke's house, and there saw *Twelfth Night* acted well, though it be but a silly play and not relating at all to the name or day. Thence Mr. Battersby (the apothecary), his wife and I and mine by coach together and setting him down at his house, he paying his share, my wife and I home, and found all well, only myself somewhat vexed at my wife's neglect in leaving of her scarf, waistcoat, and night-dressings in the coach today that brought us from Westminster, though I confess she did give them to me to look after, yet it was her fault not to see that I did take them out of the coach. I believe it might be as good as 25s loss or thereabouts.

Samuel Pepys, *The Diary of Samuel Pepys*, edited with additions by Henry B. Wheatley, 1893, II, 6.

2 November 1667

Up, and to the office, where busy all the morning; at noon home, and after dinner my wife and Willett and I to the King's playhouse and there saw *Henry the Fourth*; and contrary to expectations, was pleased in nothing more than in Cartwright's speaking of Falstaffe's speech about 'What is honour?' The house being full of Parliament-men, it being holiday with them. And it was observable how a gentleman of good habit, sitting just before us, eating of some fruit in the midst of the play, did drop down as dead, being choked; but with much ado, Orange Moll did thrust her finger down his throat, and brought him to life again.

The Diary of Samuel Pepys, VII, 183–4.

11 May 1668

And after dinner, I out and took a coach and called Mercer, and she and I to the Duke of York's playhouse and there saw *The Tempest*; and between two acts, I went out to Mr. Harris and got him to repeat to me the words of the Echo,* while I writ them down, having tried in the play to have wrote them; but when I had done it, having done it without looking upon my paper, I find I could not read the blacklead. But now I have got the words clear and, in going in thither, had the pleasure to see the Actors in their several dresses, especially the seamen and monster, which were very droll: so into the play again. But there happened one thing which vexed me, which is, that the orange-woman did come in the pit and challenge me for twelve oranges which she delivered by my order at a late play at night, to give to some ladies in a box, which was wholly untrue, but yet she swore it to be true. But, however, I did deny it and did not pay her; but, for quiet, did buy 4s. worth of oranges of her, at 6d. a piece.

The Diary of Samuel Pepys, VIII, 13.

21 December 1668

Thence to the Duke's playhouse and saw *Macbeth*. The King and Court there; and we sat just under them and my Lady Castlemayne, and close to the woman that comes into the pit, a kind of loose gossip, that pretends to be like her, and is so, something. And my wife, by my troth, appeared I think as pretty as any of them; I never thought so much before; and

*Ariel echoes Ferdinand.

so did Talbot and W. Hewer, as they said, I heard, to one another. The King and the Duke of York minded me, and smiled upon me at the handsome woman near me: but it vexed me to see Moll Davis, in the box over his and Lady Castlemayne's head, look down upon the King and he up to her; and so did my Lady Castlemayne once, to see who it was; but when she saw her, she looked like fire; which troubled me.

The Diary of Samuel Pepys, VIII, 185.

•

Davenant's version of *Macbeth*, published in 1674, was an archetypal Restoration adaptation of Shakespeare.

And now follows V, iii, but this Macbeth is not Shakespeare's. Vanished is that fierce contumely which reveals the extremity of his bewildered spirit: we get instead such insipidities as

> Now Friend, what means thy change of Countenance?

For:

> The divell damne thee blacke, thou cream-fac'd Loon:
> Where got'st thou that Goose-looke?

Hazelton Spencer, *Shakespeare Improved*, 1927, p. 165.

Affrays often occurred in the theatre during the Restoration era. One such happened during a performance of *Macbeth* on Saturday, 28 August 1675.

At the Acting of this Tragedy, on the Stage, I saw a real one acted in the Pit; I mean the Death of Mr. *Scroop*, who received his death's wound from the late Sir *Thomas Armstrong*, and died presently after he was remov'd to a House opposite to the Theatre, in *Dorset-Garden*.

Gerard Langbaine, *English Dramatick Poets*, 1691, p. 460.

Colley Cibber

Actor, manager and playwright, 1671–1757

As it has been always judg'd their natural interest, where there are two theatres, to do one another as much mischief as they can, you may imagine it could not be long before this hostile policy shew'd itself in action. It happen'd, upon our having information on a Saturday morning that the Tuesday after *Hamlet* was intended to be acted at the other house, where it had not yet been seen, our merry menaging actors (for they were now in a manner left to govern themselves) resolv'd at any rate to steal a march upon the enemy, and take possession of the same play the day before them. Accordingly, *Hamlet* was given out that night to be acted with us on Monday. The notice of this sudden enterprize soon reach'd the other house, who in my opinion too much regarded it; for they shorten'd their first orders, and resolv'd that *Hamlet* should to *Hamlet* be opposed on the same day; whereas, had they given notice in their bills that the same play would have been acted by them the day after, the town would have been in no doubt which house they should have reserved themselves for; ours must certainly have been empty, and theirs, with more honour, have been crowded. Experience, many years after, in like cases, has convinced me that this would have been the more laudable conduct. But be that as it may; when in their Monday's bills it was seen that *Hamlet* was up against us, our consternation was terrible, to find that so hopeful a project was frustrated. In this distress, Powel, who was our commanding officer, and whose enterprising head wanted nothing but skill to carry him through the most desperate attempts; for, like others of his cast, he had murder'd many a hero only to get into his cloaths. This Powel, I say, immediately called a council of war, where the question was, whether he should fairly face the enemy, or make a retreat to some other play of more probable safety? It was soon resolved that to act *Hamlet* against *Hamlet* would be certainly throwing away the play, and disgracing themselves to little or no audience. To conclude, Powel, who was vain enough to envy Betterton as his rival, proposed to change plays with them, and that as they had given out the *Old Batchelor*, and had chang'd it for *Hamlet* against us, we should give up our *Hamlet* and turn the *Old Batchelor* upon them. This motion was agreed to, *nemine contradicente*; but upon enquiry, it was found that there were not two persons among them who had ever acted in that play: but that objection, it seems (though all the parts were to be study'd in six hours), was soon got over; Powel had an equivalent, *in petto*, that would balance any deficiency on that score, which was, that he would play the 'Old Batchelor' himself, and mimick Betterton throughout the whole part. This happy thought was approv'd with delight and applause, as whatever can be suppos'd to ridicule merit generally gives joy to those that want it. Accordingly the bills were chang'd, and at the bottom inserted:

'The part of the Old Batchelor to be perform'd
in imitation of the original.'

Printed books of the play were sent for in haste, and every actor had to pick out of it the part he had chosen: thus, while they were each of them chewing the morsel they had most mind to, some one happening to cast his eye over the Dramatis Personae, found that the main matter was still forgot, that nobody had been thought of for the part of Alderman Fondlewife. Here were all aground agen, nor was it to be conceiv'd who could make the least tolerable shift with it. This character had been so admirably acted by Dogget, that though it is only seen in the fourth act, it may be no dispraise to the play to say it probably ow'd the greatest part of its success to his performance. But, as the case was now desperate, any resource was better than none. Somebody must swallow the bitter pill, or the play must die. At last it was recollected that I had been heard to say in my wild way of talking, what a vast mind I had to play Nykin, by which name the character was more frequently call'd. Notwithstanding they were thus distress'd about the disposal of this part, most of them shook their heads at my being mentioned for it; yet Powel, who was resolv'd at all hazards to fall upon Betterton, and having no concern for what might become of any one that serv'd his ends or purpose, order'd me to be sent for; and, as he naturally lov'd to set other people wrong, honestly said before I came, 'If the fool has a mind to blow himself up at once, let us ev'n give him a clear stage for it.' Accordingly the part was put into my hands between eleven and twelve that morning, which I durst not refuse, because others were as much straitned in time for study as myself. But I had this casual advantage of most of them; that having so constantly observ'd Dogget's performance, I wanted but little trouble to make me perfect in the words; so that when it came to my turn to rehearse, while others read their parts from their books, I had put mine in my pocket, and went thro' the first scene without it; and though I was more abash'd to rehearse so remarkable a part before the actors (which is natural to most young people) than to act before an audience, yet some of the better-natur'd encouraged me so far as to say they did not think I should make an ill figure in it. To conclude, the curiosity to see Betterton mimick'd drew us a pretty good audience, and Powel (as far as applause is a proof of it) was allow'd to have burlesqu'd him very well. As I have question'd the certain value of applause, I hope I may venture with less vanity to say how particular a share I had of it in the same play.

Colley Cibber,
An Apology For The Life of Mr. Colley Cibber,
ed. Robert Lowe, 1889, I, 203–8.

Mrs. Bellamy tells us that she had the following anecdote from Colley Cibber – as Mrs. Mountfort during the time of her disorder was not outrageous, she was not placed under any rigourous confinement, but was suffered to walk about her house – one day in a lucid interval she asked what play was to be performed that evening? and was told it was to be *Hamlet* – whilst she was on the stage, she had acted Ophelia with great applause – the recollection struck her, and with all that cunning which is frequently allied to insanity, she found means to elude the care of her attendants and got to the theatre, where concealing herself till the scene when Ophelia was to make her appearance in her mad state, she pushed on the stage before the person who played the character that night, and exhibited a far more perfect representation of madness, than the utmost exertions of theatrical art could do – she was in truth *Ophelia herself*, to the amazement of the performers, as well as of the audience – nature having made this last effort, her vital powers failed her, and she died soon after.

John Genest, *Some Account of the English Stage from the Restoration in 1660 to 1830*, 1832, II, 659.

Thomas Betterton

Actor, 1635–1710

I have lately been told, by a gentleman who has frequently seen Betterton perform Hamlet, that he observed his countenance, which was naturally ruddy and sanguine, in the scene of the third act where his father's ghost appears, through the violent and sudden emotion of amazement and horror, turn, instantly, on the sight of his father's spirit, as pale as his neckcloth; when his whole body seemed to be affected with a tremor inexpressible; so that, had his father's ghost actually risen before him, he could not have been seized with more real agonies. And this was felt so strongly by the audience, that the blood seemed to shudder in their veins likewise; and they, in some measure, partook of the astonishment and horror with which they saw this excellent actor affected.

Thomas Davies, *Dramatic Miscellanies*,
1784, III, 57–8.

The story may be recalled of the old critic who, in the days of the second George when the younger men were loudly praising a recent Hamlet, proved exceptious and would allow little merit to the new interpreter of the Prince of Denmark. The chorus, however, pronounced him admirable, especially in the closet scene. Could anyone deny that his elocution was just and forcible, his carriage superb, his gestures how admirable! 'Pretty well, sir, pretty well,' quoth our *laudator temporis acti*, 'why, it was pretty well done, but then' – with a long pinch from his box – 'he did not upset the chair, sir. Now Mr. Betterton always upset the chair.' This bit of business was indeed a very old tradition, and in the illustration to Rowe's Shakespeare, 1709, the chair appears duly thrown to the ground.

Montague Summers, *The Restoration Theatre*, 1934, pp. 283–4.

Garrick, too, had his chair-trick in *Hamlet*. When the Ghost appeared between the young Dane and his mother, Garrick, starting from his chair, used always to overturn the latter, – which was differently constructed from that used by the Queen. The legs of the actor's chair were, in fact, tapered to a point, and placed so far under the seat, that it fell with a touch.

Dr [J.] Doran,
Annals of the English Stage from Thomas Betterton to Edmund Kean, ed. Robert Lowe, 1888, III, 261–2.

Barton Booth
Actor, 1681–1733

Booth was noted for his Ghost in *Hamlet*, from 1708 on.

With Wilks's general talents for Tragedy, there were some parts that he was unequal to; and in particular the *Ghost* in *Hamlet*. One day at rehearsal, Booth took the liberty to jest with him upon it. 'Why, Bob,' says he, 'I thought last night you wanted to play at fisty cuffs with me (Booth played Hamlet to his Ghost), you bullied me so, who, by the bye, you ought to have revered. I remember when I acted the

Ghost with Betterton, instead of my awing him, he terrified me – But there was a divinity hung round that man.'

. . . He was, beside, always particularly well dressed for the character, even to the soles of his shoes, which, from being covered with *felt*, made no noise in walking on the stage, which he crossed as if he slid over it, and which strongly corresponded with the ideas we have of an incorporeal being.

William Cooke, *Memoirs of Charles Macklin, Comedian*, 1804, pp. 356, 376.

John Dennis

Critic and playwright, 1657–1734

Dennis is credited with introducing an improved method of stage thunder, as also with the phrase 'to steal one's thunder'.

Mr. Dennis happened once to go to the play, when a tragedy was acted [*Macbeth*, 1709], in which the machinery of thunder was introduced, a new artificial method of producing which he had formerly communicated to the managers. Incensed by this circumstance, he cried out in a transport of resentment, 'That is my thunder by G-d; the villains will play my thunder, but not my plays.' This gave an alarm to the pit, which he soon explained.

Theophilus Cibber, *Lives of the Poets of Great Britain and Ireland*, 1753, IV, 234.

•

Sir Richard Steele tells us (in one of the *Tatlers*) of a poor actor in his time who, having nothing to do, fell away, and became such a wretched, meagre-looking object, that he was pitched upon as a proper person to represent the starved apothecary in *Romeo and Juliet*. He did this so much to the life that he was repeatedly called upon to play it; but his person improving with his circumstances, he was in a short time rendered unfit to play it with the same effect as before, and laid aside. Having no other resources, he accordingly fell away again with the loss of his part, and was again called upon to appear in it with his former reputation.

William Hazlitt, *The Examiner*, 13 October 1816;
Hazlitt on Theatre, ed. William Archer and
Robert Lowe, I, p. 105.

A most serious riot occurred at the Portugal Street Theatre in 1721 through the practice of allowing certain privileged persons to sit upon the stage during the performance . . . One night, in a principal scene of *Macbeth*, a nobleman crossed from one side of the stage to the other, in front of the actors, to speak to a friend; when Rich remonstrated with him upon the impropriety of such behaviour my lord struck him in the face. Rich and Quin drew their swords, the rest of the company supported them, and the beaux took the offender's side. But the players proving too strong, their foes were driven out of the theatre. Reinforced, the rioters returned, smashed the handsome mirrors that lined the proscenium, threw torches among the scenery, tore up the seats, and it was not until the military were called out that the disturbance was quelled. From that time a fashion, which had been introduced by Charles II, of posting a guard on each side the stage was revived, and partly survives to the present day in the soldiers that attend the performances at Drury Lane and Covent Garden.

H. Barton Baker,
History of the London Stage and its Famous Players, 1576–1903, 1904, pp. 111–12

A noteworthy benefit performance of *The Tempest* was staged at Drury Lane on Friday, 28 November 1740, 'By Command of His Royal Highness the Prince of Wales'.

The Tempest BT. the brave and unfortunate crew [of the *Prince of Orange*], belonging to Capt. [John] Peddie, who (after having clear'd themselves by the most gallant behaviour from a Spanish privateer) were shipwreck'd in a tempest in Margate Road [on 1 November], and stood on the wreck upwards of twelve hours, with the sea beating over them, before they were relieved. And for the benefit of the widow of the boatswain, killed in the engagement.

Charles Beecher Hogan,
Shakespeare in the Theatre 1701–1800: A Record of Performances in London 1701–1750, 1952, I, 56.

Charles Macklin

Actor, c. 1700–1797

Macklin's great success was as Shylock, a part he played for almost fifty years. His first performance was on 14 February 1741, at Drury Lane.

The long-expected night at last arrived, and the House was crowded, from top to bottom, with the first company in town. The two front rows of the pit, as usual, were full of critics, 'Who, Sir, (said the veteran) I eyed through the slit of the curtain, and was glad to see there, as I wished, in such a cause, to be tried by a *special jury*. When I made my appearance in the green-room, dressed for the part, with my red hat on my head, my piqued beard, loose black gown, &c.

and with a confidence which I never before assumed, the performers all stared at one another, and evidently with a stare of disappointment. Well, Sir, hitherto, all was right – till the last bell rung – then, I confess, my heart began to beat a little: however, I mustered up all the courage I could, and, recommending my cause to Providence, threw myself boldly on the stage, and was received by one of the loudest thunders of applause I ever before experienced.

'The opening scenes being rather tame and level, I could not expect much applause; but I found myself well listened to – I could hear distinctly, in the pit, the words "Very well – very well, indeed! – This man seems to know what he is about," &c. &c. These encomiums warmed me, but did not overset me – I knew where I should have the pull, which was in the third act, and reserved myself accordingly. At this period I threw out all my fire; and as the contrasted passions of joy for the Merchant's losses, and grief for the elopement of Jessica, open a fine field for an actor's powers, I had the good fortune to please beyond my warmest expectations – The whole house was in an uproar of applause – and I was obliged to pause between the speeches, to give it vent, so as to be heard. When I went behind the scenes after this act, the Manager met me, and complimented me very highly on my performance, and significantly added, "Macklin, you was right at last." My brethren in the green-room joined in his eulogium, but with different views – He was thinking of the increase of his treasury – they only for saving appearances – wishing at the same time that I had broke my neck in the attempt. The *trial scene* wound up the fulness of my reputation: here I was well listened to; and here I made such a silent yet forcible impression on my audience, that I retired from this great attempt most perfectly satisfied.

'On my return to the green-room, after the play was over, it was crowded with nobility and critics, who all complimented me in the warmest and most unbounded manner; and the situation I felt myself in, I must confess, was one of the most flattering and intoxicating of my whole life. No money, no title, could purchase what I felt: And let no man tell me after this, what Fame will not inspire a man to do, and how far the attainment of it will not remunerate his greatest labours. By G-d, Sir, though I was not worth fifty pounds in the world at that time, yet, let me tell you, I was *Charles the Great* for that night.'

William Cooke, *Memoirs of Charles Macklin*, 1804, pp. 92–4.

Macklin was very particular in *Shylock*, so much so, that he requested Bobby Bates, who performed the part of *Tubal*, not to speak until he saw him standing on a certain spot; 'nay,' said Macklin, 'not till you see me place my right foot on this nail,' (pointing with his stick to the head of a large nail which was driven into the stage). Bobby promised to remember the old man's instruction; and, that he might have a better view of the nail, he marked it in a conspicuous manner with a piece of chalk. At night, Macklin had forgotten the nail; therefore, when *Tubal* entered, and remained, for some time, without speaking, Macklin exclaimed, in an under voice, 'Why the devil don't you speak?' – 'Sir,' replied Bobby, '*put your right foot upon the nail.*' This so disconcerted the veteran that it was with great difficulty he finished the part.

Richard Ryan,
Dramatic Table Talk, 1825–30, II, 57–8.

The actors themselves were evidently no less reluctant to accept his [Macklin's] ideas. An exception was the young and beautiful Mrs. Hartley, fifty years his junior. She had earlier played Lady Macbeth opposite Smith, to whom she was strongly attracted, but good-natured curiosity induced her to pay attention to the older actor. Others were not so tractable, however. Dunstall and Quick, both low comedians, had been cast as witches, and they were prepared to play them in the accepted fashion as figures of fun rather than the dark embodiments of man's fate. The tension at rehearsals was not lessened by Macklin's constant interruptions and anguished exclamations. 'Sir, Sir!' he would cry. 'Do you know what you are about? None of your hackneyed turns and practises with me! Throw Garrick to the dogs! I'll have none of him. He is for Nature and Shakespeare; I am for Shakespeare and Nature! Hark you, ye witches! Manage your broomsticks with dignity and be damned to you! Ride through the air like gentlewomen, and as if mounted on so many Pegasuses!'

William W. Appleton,
Charles Macklin: An Actor's Life, 1960, pp. 176–7.

Macklin continued to act until an advanced age. His memory failed him during a performance of *The Merchant of Venice* in January 1788, and he stepped forward to address the audience.

Ladies and Gentlemen: Within these very few hours I have been seized with a terror of mind I never in my life felt before; it has totally destroyed my corporeal as well as mental faculties. I must therefore request your patience this night, a request which an old man of eighty-nine years may hope is not unreasonable. Should it be granted you may depend, that this will be the last night, unless my health shall be entirely re-established, of my ever appearing before you in so ridiculous a situation.

Francis Congreve,
Authentic Memoirs of the late Mr. Charles Macklin, Comedian, 1798, pp. 55–6.

His last attempt on the stage was on the 7th of May following [1789], in the character of Shylock, for his own benefit. Here his imbecilities were previously foreseen, or at least dreaded, by the manager; but who, knowing the state of Macklin's finances, gave, with his usual liberality, this indulgence to his age and necessities, and, to prevent the disappointment of the audience (who, he knew, from long experience, were always ready to assist in those liberal indulgences to an old and meritorious servant), he had the late Mr. Ryder understudied in the part, ready dressed to supply Macklin's deficiencies if necessary. The precaution afterwards proved so.

When Macklin had dressed himself for the part, which he did with his usual accuracy, he went into the Green Room, but with such a 'lack-lustre looking eye' as plainly indicated his inability to perform; and coming up to the late Mrs. Pope, said, 'My dear, are you to play tonight?' 'Good God! To be sure I am, Sir. Why, don't you see I am dressed for Portia?' 'Ah! Very true; I had forgot. But who is to play Shylock?' The imbecile tone of his voice and the inanity of the look, with which the last question was asked, caused a melancholy sensation in all who heard it. At last Mrs. Pope, rousing herself, said, 'Why you, to be sure; are you not dressed for the part?' He then seemed to recollect himself, and, putting his hand to his forehead pathetically exclaimed, 'God help me – my memory, I am afraid, has left me.'

He, however, after this, went upon the Stage, and delivered two or three speeches of Shylock in a manner that evidently proved he did not understand what he was repeating. After a while he recovered himself a little, and seemed to make an effort to rouse himself; but in vain – Nature could assist him no further; and, after pausing some time as if considering what to do, he then came forward, and informed the audience, 'That he now found he was unable to proceed in the part, and hoped they would accept Mr. Ryder as his substitute, who was already prepared to finish it.' The audience accepted his apology with a mixed applause of indulgence and commiseration, and he retired from the stage forever.

William Cooke,
Memoirs of Charles Macklin, 1804, pp. 315–17.

•

All's Well That Ends Well, of which no performance is recorded before 1741, was revived in 1742 at Drury Lane.

All's well that ends well was termed, by the players, the unfortunate comedy, from the disagreeable accidents which fell out several times during the acting of it . . . Milward, who acted the King, is said to have caught a distemper which proved fatal to him, by wearing, in this part, a too light and airy suit of clothes, which he put on after his supposed recovery. He felt himself seized with a shivering; and was asked, by one of the players, how he found himself? 'How is it possible for me,' he said, with some pleasantry, 'to be sick, when I have such a physician as Mrs. Woffington?'

Thomas Davies,
Dramatic Miscellanies, 1783, II, 9, 7.

James Quin
Actor, 1693–1766

Quin plays *Coriolanus* at Covent Garden, January 1749.

The following ludicrous incident occurred during a Rehearsal of *Coriolanus*, while it was preparing for the benefit of Thomson's sisters. Quin's pronunciation was of the Old School. In this Garrick had made an alteration. The one pronounced the letter *a* open, the other sounded it like an *e*, which occasioned the following mistake. In the scene where the Roman ladies come in procession, to solicit Coriolanus to return to Rome, they are attended by the Tribunes, and the Centurions of the Volscian Army, bearing *fasces*, their Ensigns of authority. They are ordered by the Hero, the part of which was enacted by Quin, to lower them, as a token of respect. But the men who personated the Centurions, imagining, through Quin's mode of enunciation, that he said their *faces*, instead of the *fasces*, all bowed their heads together.

Richard Ryan,
Dramatic Table Talk, 1825–30, II, 120–1.

•

An early performance of *Othello* in Williamsburg, Virginia.

The Emperor of the Cherokee nation with his Empress and their son, the young Prince, attended by several of his warriors and Great Men and their Ladies, were received at the Palace by his Honour the Governor, attended by such of the Council as were in Town, on Thursday, the 9th inst., with all the marks of Courtesy and Friendship, and were that evening entertained at the theatre with The Tragedy of 'Othello' and a Pantomime performance which gave them great surprise, as did the fighting with naked swords on the Stage, which occasioned the Empress to order some about her to go and prevent them killing one another.

Letter to the *Maryland Gazette* of 9 November 1752, quoted in Arthur Hornblow, *A History of the Theatre in America*, Philadelphia, 1919, I, 87.

David Garrick

Actor, 1717–1779

Garrick, with all his brilliant genius, was a very methodical actor. When he had once settled in what is technically called the 'business' of a part, he never altered it. In the play-scene, when he satisfies himself that he has detected the guilt of the *King*, he wound up his burst of exultation at the close by three flourishes of his pocket-handkerchief over his head, as he paced the stage backwards and forwards. It was once remarked as an extraordinary deviation, that he added a fourth flourish.

John William Cole,
The Life and Theatrical Times of Charles Kean, FSA, 1859, I, 282–3.

Garrick's manner of speaking his lines was sometimes criticised. Sterne satirises the extreme formalist view of Garrick.

'And how did Garrick speak the soliloquy last night?' 'Oh against all rule, My Lord, Most ungrammatically! Betwixt the substantive and the adjective, which should agree together in number, case, and gender, he made a breech thus –, stopping as if the point wanted settling; and betwixt the nominative case, which your Lordship knows must govern the verb, he suspended his voice in the Epilogue a dozen times, three seconds and three fifths by a stop-watch, my Lord, each time!' – 'Admirable grammarian! But in suspending his voice was the sense suspended likewise? Did no expression of attitude, or countenance fill up the chasm? Was the eye silent? Did you narrowly look?' 'I looked only at the stop-watch, My Lord.' – 'Excellent observer!'

Lawrence Sterne,
Tristram Shandy, 1761, III, Chapter XII.

The feature of the 1750–1 season was the Battle of the Theatres. On 28 September, *Romeo and Juliet* opened at two theatres. Drury Lane had Garrick as Romeo and Miss Bellamy as Juliet; Covent Garden had Spranger Barry as Romeo and Mrs Cibber as Juliet. The two productions played concurrently for twelve nights, which was then considered a wonder, after which Covent Garden broke off and Garrick played a victorious thirteenth night. The leading actors were considered well matched.

Perhaps, after all, the truest idea of the two Romeos may be gathered from the remark of a lady who did not pretend to be a critic, and who was guided by her feelings. 'Had I been Juliet,' she said, 'to Garrick's Romeo, – so ardent and impassioned was he, I should have expected that he would have *come up* to me in the balcony; but had I been Juliet to Barry's Romeo, so tender, so eloquent, and so seductive was he, I should certainly have *gone down* to him!'

Dr [J.] Doran,
Annals of the English Stage from Thomas Betterton to Edmund Kean, ed. Robert Lowe, 1888, II, 123.

Garrick claimed the victory, in a letter to the Countess of Burlington dated 13 October 1750.

Madam,

I can give Yr Ladp the Satisfaction, & I flatter Myself that it will be so to You, of assuring you that ye Battle is at last Ended, & in our favour – our Antagonists yielded last thursday Night & we play'd ye Same Play (Romeo & Juliet) on ye Fryday to a very full house to very great applause; Mr. Barry & Mrs. Cibber came incog to see Us, & I am very well-assur'd they receiv'd no little Mortification . . .

The Letters of David Garrick, ed. David M. Little and George M. Kahrl, 1963, I, 156.

. . . we have heard it mentioned that once, when Garrick was in the middle of the mad scene [in *King Lear*], his crown of straw came off, which circumstance, though it would have been fatal to a common actor, did not produce the smallest interruption, or even notice in the house. On another occasion, while he was kneeling to repeat the curse, the first row in the pit stood up in order to see him better; the second row, not willing to lose the precious moments by remonstrating, stood up too; and so, by a tacit movement, the entire pit rose to hear the withering imprecation, while the whole passed in such cautious silence that you might have heard a pin drop.

William Hazlitt, *London Magazine*, VI, June 1820, reprinted in *Hazlitt on Theatre*, ed. William Archer and Robert Lowe, pp. 190–1.

When Garrick first came upon the stage, one very sultry evening in the month of May, and performed the character of Lear in the first four acts he received the customary tokens of applause; at the conclusion of the fifth, when he wept over the body of Cordelia, every eye caught the soft infection, big round tears ran down every cheek. At this interesting moment, to the astonishment of all present, his face assumed a new character, and his whole frame appeared agitated by a new passion; it was not tragic, for he was evidently endeavouring to suppress a laugh. In a few seconds, the attendant nobles appeared to be affected in the same manner; and the beauteous Cordelia, who reclined upon a crimson couch, opening her eyes to see what occasioned the interruption, leaped from her sofa, and with the Majesty of England, and the gallant Kent, ran laughing off the stage. The audience could not account for so strange a termination of a tragedy in any other way than by supposing the cast to be seized by a sudden frenzy; but their risibility had a different source.

A Whitechapel butcher, seated in the centre of the first bench of the pit, was accompanied by his mastiff, who, being accustomed to sit on the same seat as his master at home, thought naturally enough that he might enjoy the same privilege here. The butcher sat back, and the quadruped, finding a fair opening, got upon the bench, and fixing his forepaws on the rails of the orchestra, peered at the performers with as upright an head, and as grave an air as the most sagacious critic of the day. The corpulent slaughterman was made of 'melting stuff' and, being not accustomed to a play-house heat, found himself much oppressed by the weight of a large and well-powdered Sunday peruke, which, for the gratification of cooling his head, he pulled off, and placed on the head of the mastiff. The dog, being in so conspicuous a situation, caught the eye of Garrick and the other performers. A mastiff in a church-warden's wig was too much; it would have provoked laughter in Lear himself at the moment he was most distressed – no wonder that it had such an effect upon his representative.

Richard Ryan,
Dramatic Table Talk, 1825–30, II, 120–1.

Before we leave the discussion of human encumbrances on the stage, we may state that the two grenadiers still continued on guard at the stage-doors throughout the Garrick period . . . I cannot refrain from referring to the oft-told tale of Garrick and these guardians of the peace. According to the legend, one of the grenadiers was so overcome by the acting of Garrick as Lear that he fainted in full view of the audience; Garrick, deeply touched by this tribute to his powers, rewarded the fellow with a guinea. Naturally, word of this generosity spread, and the next night of Garrick's acting another guard dropped down at his post. Only that night Garrick was acting a comedy!

George C.D. Odell,
Shakespeare From Betterton To Irving,
1921, I, 411–12.

As I take leave of Garrick, I remember the touching scene which occurred on the last night but one of his public performances. His farewell to the stage was made in a comic character; but he and tragedy parted for ever the night before. On that occasion he played Lear to the Cordelia of Miss Younge. As the curtain descended, they lay on the stage hand in hand, and hand in hand they rose and went, Garrick silently leading, to his dressing-room; whither they were followed by many of the company. There stood Lear and Cordelia, still hand in hand, and mute. At last Garrick exclaimed, 'Ah, Bessie, this is the last time I shall ever be your father; the *last time*!' and he dropped her hand. Miss Younge sighed too, and replied affectionately, with a hope that before they finally parted he would kindly give her a father's blessing. Garrick took it as it was meant, seriously; and as Miss Younge bowed her head, he raised his hands, and prayed that God would bless her! Then slowly looking round, he murmured, 'May God bless you all!' and divesting himself of his Lear's dress, tragedy, and one of her most accomplished sons, were dissevered for ever!

Dr [J.] Doran,
Annals of the English Stage from Thomas Betterton to Edmund Kean, ed. Robert Lowe, 1888, II, 334.

Peg Woffington

Actress, c. 1718–1760

Peg Woffington's last appearance, 3 May 1757.

I was standing near the wing as Mrs. Woffington in Rosalind, and Mrs. Vincent in Celia, were going on the stage in the first act. Mrs. Woffington ironically said she was glad to have that opportunity of congratulating me on my stage success; and did not doubt, but such merit would insure me an engagement the following winter. I bowed but made her no answer – I knew her dislike to me, and was humiliated sufficiently, and needed not any slight to sink me lower. For then, and not till then, adversity had taught me to know myself. She went through Rosalind for four acts without my perceiving she was in the least disordered, but in the fifth she complained of great indisposition. I offered her my arm, which she graciously accepted; I thought she looked softened in her behaviour, and had less of the *hauteur*. When she came off at the quick change of dress, she again complained of being ill; but got accoutered and returned to finish the part, and pronounced in the epilogue speech, 'If it be true that good wine needs no bush – it is as true that a good play needs no epilogue,' etc. etc. – But when arrived at – 'If I were among you I would kiss as many of you as had beards that pleased me' her voice broke, she faltered, endeavoured to go on, but could not proceed – then in a voice of tremor screamed, O God! O God! tottered to the stage door speechless, where she was caught. The audience of course applauded till she was out of sight, and then sunk into awful looks of astonishment, both young and old, to see one of the most handsome women of the age, a favourite principal actress, and who had for several seasons given high entertainment, struck so suddenly by the hand of death in such a situation of time and place, and in her prime of life, being then about forty-four. She was given over that night, and for several days; but so far recovered as to linger till near the year 1760, but existed as a mere skeleton; *sans* teeth, *sans* eyes, *sans* taste, *sans* every thing. – Vain is Beauty's gaudy flower!

Tate Wilkinson, *Memoirs*, 1790.

Susannah Cibber

Actress, 1714–1766

'I was never more astonished in my life,' declared an anonymous correspondent to the *Theatrical Review* in 1763, 'than at an action of Mrs Cibber's. As that lady sat upon the stage with Hamlet at her feet, in the 3rd act she rose up three several times and made as many courtesies – and those very low ones – to some ladies in the boxes. Pray, good sir, ask her in what part of the play it is said that the Danish Ophelia . . . is acquainted with so many British Ladies?' The ladies before whom Susannah prostrated herself had come expressly to see her, had paid handsomely for their boxes, perhaps as much as £100 for a chair on the stage, and they may well have expected the recipient of such ostentatious favour to acknowledge their presence.

Mary Nash,
The Provoked Wife: The Life and Times of Susannah Cibber, 1977, p. 269.

•

Last words ought to be received with great caution. A characteristic sentence may be pronounced by a man, and repeated as his 'last words', when in reality he did not die until long after they were spoken. The awful significance claimed for 'last words' can be imparted only by death immediately following their delivery, as in the case of Paterson, who dropped dead in Moody's arms, after repeating from *Measure for Measure* the lines –

> Reason thus with life:
> If I do lose thee, I do lose a thing
> That none but fools would keep: a breath thou art.

W. Clark Russell,
Representative Actors, 1888, p. 203.

John Henderson

Actor, 1747–1785

In November of that year – 1778 – he played Falstaff in a performance of the first part of *King Henry IV*. The day was Saturday the 18th. Bath society had been shocked a few days previously to hear of the death of a French nobleman, the Vicomte du Barré, in a duel on Claverton Down; the Vicomte was residing temporarily in Royal Crescent, and had been shot and killed by a friend and accomplice after they had quarrelled over a sum of money won at cards. The duel had taken place on the previous Wednesday; and when, at the theatre, Henderson came to Falstaff's lines 'What is honour? A word. What is that word honour? What is that honour? A trim reckoning! Who hath it?' he paused deliberately, and went on, 'He that died on Wednesday!' The words, of course, created a sensation in the packed house. Many in the audience believed that the last phrase was an impromptu addition. They were wrong: Henderson kept strictly to the text of the play. It was his sense of timing that made the passage so dramatically effective.

William Lowndes,
The Theatre Royal at Bath, 1982, p. 24.

Henderson one night got imperfect in Benedick. It was in his soliloquy in the second act, in Leonato's orchard.

> I do much wonder, that one man, seeing how much another man is a fool, when he dedicates his behaviours to love, will, after he hath laughed at such shallow follies in others, become the argument of his own scorn, by falling in love!

Henderson, after stating his first position, and uttering the separated word *will*, could not supply the following expressions, and made a sudden stop. The prompter, knowing his actor, and supposing it as impossible for the words of Benedick to escape from Henderson's memory, as from the prompt-book itself, had, for a few minutes, quitted his seat at the wing, and in course did not perceive the dilemma. Henderson began again, and stopt precisely at the same word: he then became vexed, and loudly called out *give me the word*. Upon this the audience gave him the usual signs of their favour, and he rose from the seat on which he reclined, and bowed. By this time the prompter, Wild, was returned to his place, the words wanted were given, and he proceeded as usual.

James Boaden,
Memoirs of the Life of John Philip Kemble,
1825, I, 249–50.

Samuel Reddish

Actor, 1735–1785

On one occasion, at Covent Garden, when he was performing as *Hamlet*, the player (Whitfield) of *Laertes*, in the Fencing Scene, made an awkward lunge with his rapier, which removed the *Prince's* wig, showing him to be bald. The mortification of Reddish at this occurrence was so afflicting that, according to his friend John Taylor, it eventually caused mental derangement.

William Winter,
Shakespeare on the Stage, Third Series, 1916, p. 76.

Samuel Reddish's last appearance on stage (5 May 1779).

. . . when the late Mr. Reddish's indisposition of mind rendered him incapable of fulfilling his duty at the theatre, and he was supported by the Fund, some of his friends prevailed on the manager to grant him a benefit – the play was *Cymbeline* – he was to pass an hour previous to his performance at a house where I was asked to meet him – he came into the room with the step of an Idiot, his eye wandering and his whole countenance vacant – I congratulated him on his being well enough to perform – 'Yes Sir' replied he 'and in the Garden Scene I shall astonish you!' – 'In the Garden Scene Mr. Reddish, I thought you were to play Posthumus' – 'No Sir I play Romeo' – 'My good man' said the Gentleman of the house, 'you play Posthumus' – 'do I?' replied he, 'I am sorry for it; however, what must be, must be' – the Gentleman who went with him to the theatre, for he was not capable of walking without a guide, told me, that his mind was so imprest with the character of Romeo, that he was reciting it all the way; and when he came into the green-room it was with extreme difficulty they could persuade him that he was to play any other part – when the time came for his appearance they pushed him on the stage, fearing he would begin with a speech of Romeo – with the same expectation, I stood in the Pit close to the Orchestra, and being so near, I had a perfect view of his face – the instant he came in sight of the audience, his recollection seemed to return, his countenance resumed meaning, his eye appeared lighted up, he made the bow of modest respect, and went through the scene much better than I had ever seen him – on his return to the green-room, the image of Romeo came again into his mind, nor did he lose it till his second appearance, when the moment he had the cue, he went through the scene as Posthumus, and in this weak state of mind, acted the whole character better than he had ever done before, his manner was less assuming and more natural.

Ireland, *Life of Henderson*, quoted in John Genest, *Some Account of the English Stage from the Restoration in 1660 to 1830*, 1832, VI, 102–4.

Mary Robinson

Actress, 1748–1800

The liaison between Mrs Mary Robinson and the young Prince of Wales began at a performance of *The Winter's Tale*, at Drury Lane.

Mrs. Mary Robinson left the stage at the close of this season – On Dec. the 3d [1779] the Winter's Tale was acted by command of their Majesties – when Mrs. Robinson went into the Greenroom dressed as Perdita, ['Gentleman'] Smith exclaimed 'By Jove you will make a conquest of the Prince for you look handsomer than ever' – Smith proved a true prophet, and some few days after, she received, through the hands of a Nobleman, a letter addressed to Perdita, and with peculiar propriety signed Florizel – many other letters passed, and in consequence of Florizel's attachment, she quitted the stage – the particulars of this connexion may be seen in her Memoirs – Florizel was never remarkable for the constancy of his attachments, and finally separated from her in the course of 1781 – in 1788 she obtained a grant of £500 a year, to which she was justly entitled, as she had quitted a lucrative profession at the particular request of Florizel . . .

John Genest,
Some Account of the English Stage from the Restoration in 1660 to 1830, 1832, VI, 136–7.

•

. . . *The Gazetteer and New Daily Advertiser*, September 22, 1783, notes the discovery 'during the repair of Drury-lane Theatre in the summer' of

> a human scull in the earth under the stage . . . An old scene shifter unravelled the mystery, by declaring it was no other than Yorick's scull used in Hamlet, and that he remembered it being lost many years since in Mr. Garrick's time.

The omission of the Gravedigger's Scene in Garrick's version of the play may perhaps explain how so important a property could have been mislaid.

Arthur Colby Sprague,
Shakespeare and the Actors: The Stage Business in His Plays, 1660–1905, 1944, p. 174.

Dr Samuel Johnson

Writer, critic and lexicographer, 1709–1784

Johnson, indeed, had thought more upon the subject of acting than might be generally supposed. Talking of it one day to Mr Kemble, he said, 'Are you, Sir, one of those enthusiasts who believe yourself transformed into the very character you represent?' Upon Mr Kemble's answering that he had never felt so strong a persuasion himself; 'To be sure not, Sir, (said Johnson;) the thing is impossible. And if Garrick really believed himself to be that monster, Richard the Third, he deserved to be hanged every time he performed it.'

Boswell's Life of Johnson, ed. G. Birkbeck Hill, 1887, II, 243–4.

James William Dodd

Actor, singer and manager, ?1740 – 1796

Few now remember Dodd. What an Aguecheek the stage lost in him! Lovegrove, who came nearest to the old actors, revived the character some few seasons ago, and made it sufficiently grotesque; but Dodd was *it*, as it came out of nature's hands. It might be said to remain *in puris naturalibus*. In expressing slowness of apprehension this actor surpassed all others. You could see the first dawn of an idea stealing slowly over his countenance, till it cleared up at last to the fulness of a twilight conception – its highest meridian. He seemed to keep back his intellect, as some have had the power to retard their pulsation. The balloon takes less time in filling, than it took to cover the expansion of his broad moony face over all its quarters with expression. A glimmer of understanding would appear in a corner of his eye, and for lack of fuel go out again. A part of his forehead would catch a little intelligence, and be a long time communicating it to the remainder.

I am ill at dates, but I think it is now better than five and twenty years ago that walking in the gardens of Gray's Inn . . . taking my afternoon solace on a summer day upon the aforesaid terrace, a comely, sad personage came towards me, whom, from his grave air and deportment, I judged to be one of the old Benchers of the Inn. He had a serious thoughtful forehead, and seemed to be in meditations of mortality. As I have an instinctive awe of old Benchers, I was passing him with that sort of subindicative token of respect which one is apt to demonstrate towards a venerable stranger, and which rather denotes an inclination to greet him, than any positive motion of the body to that effect – a species of humility and will-worship which I observe, nine times out of ten, rather puzzles than pleases the person it is offered to – when the face turning full upon me strangely identified itself with that of Dodd. Upon close inspection I was not mistaken. But could this sad thoughtful countenance be the same vacant face of folly which I had hailed so often under circumstances of gaiety; which I had never seen without a smile, or recognized but as the usher of mirth; that looked out so formally flat in Foppington, so frothingly pert in Tattle, so impotently busy in Backbite; so blankly divested of all meaning, or resolutely expressive of none, in Acres, in Fribble, and a thousand agreeable impertinences? Was this the face – full of thought and carefulness – that had so often divested itself at will of every trace of either to give me diversion, to clear my cloudy face for two or three hours at least of its furrows? Was this the face – manly, sober, intelligent, – which I had so often despised, made mocks at, made merry with? The remembrance of the freedoms which I had taken with it came upon me with a reproach of insult. I could have asked it pardon. I thought it looked upon me with a sense of injury. There is something strange as well as sad in seeing actors – your pleasant fellows particularly – subjected to and suffering the common lot – their fortunes, their casualties, their deaths, seem to belong to the scene, their actions to be amenable to poetic justice only. We can hardly connect them with more awful responsibilities. The death of this fine actor took place shortly after this meeting. He had quitted the stage some months; and, as I learned afterwards, had been in the habit of resorting daily to these gardens almost to the day of his decease. In these serious walks probably he was divesting himself of many scenic and some real vanities – weaning himself from the frivolities of the lesser and the greater theatre – doing gentle penance for a life of no very reprehensible fooleries, – taking off by degrees the buffoon mask which he might feel he had worn too long – and rehearsing for a more solemn cast of part.

Charles Lamb, 'On Some of the Old Actors',
Essays of Elia, 1823.

●

On the 26th of December [1801], one of those disgusting scenes of barbarous riot occurred at Covent Garden, originating from the monstrous practice of carrying spirits into the theatre, and generally providing, among the lower orders, for a few hours' entertainment, as if they were to garrison a town besieged. The play was *Richard III*. The first missile that threatened execution was a *wine glass*. On the entry of Betterton, as Tressel, to Murray, who acted King Henry VI, a *quart bottle* grazed his hat; the actor took it up, and walked off the stage. The indignation of the audience burst out against the villain, who was, after an obstinate resistance, secured where he sat, in the front row of the two-shilling gallery, on the King's side. Some very unlucky alterations in the performances, from indisposition, kept up the Saturnalian licence of the rabble, and the trumpets, and the shouts of Bosworth Field, could not be heard. The actors became a sort of *Shrove Tuesday* sport to these brutes; and they enjoyed and prolonged the agile feats of Emery, who jumped away with singular misery, from the various *throws* at him, consisting of all the apples and oranges supplied by the fruit women . . .

The farce was hurried over; the ladies would not, at last, come upon the stage; the pit took part in the tumult; the lights were extinguished, and the benches were becoming unseated, when BRANDON, at the head of a few remaining soldiers, with their bayonets fixed, about *five* guardsmen, on a sudden appeared in the gallery. The glittering steel had a very calming effect upon the mischievous, and this cruel and dastardly mob slunk away in haste out of the theatre, then nearly quite dark.

James Boaden,
Memoirs of the Life of John Philip Kemble,
1825, II, 307–8.

Master Betty

Actor, the 'Young Roscius', 1791–1874

Betty reached the peak of his fame in 1804–5.

. . . if the overtaxed boy fell ill, as he did more than once, the public forgot the general social distress, the threats of invasion, war abroad and sedition at home, and evinced such painful anxiety, that bulletins were daily issued, as though the lad were king-regnant or heir-apparent.

Subsequently, Drury Lane and Covent Garden shared him

between them. In twenty-three nights, at the former house, he drew above £17,000, and this double work so doubled his popularity, that on one night, having to play Hamlet, the House of Commons, on a motion by Pitt, adjourned, and went down to the theatre to see him!

Dr [J.] Doran,
Annals of the English Stage from Thomas Betterton to Edmund Kean, ed. Robert Lowe, 1888, III, 244.

Byron shared in the Betty-mania, but came to abandon it.

. . . when I last saw him I was in raptures with his performances, but then I was sixteen – an age to which all London then condescended to subside . . . Betty is performing here, I fear, very ill, his figure is that of a hippopotamus, his face like the Bull and *mouth* on the pannels of a heavy coach, his arms are fins fattened out of shape, his voice the gargling of an Alderman with the quinsey, and his acting altogether ought to be natural, for it certainly is like nothing that *Art* has ever yet exhibited on the stage.

Letters to Lord Holland and to Lady Melbourne (Cheltenham, 10 September 1812),
Byron's Letters and Journals,
ed. Leslie A. Marchand, II (1973), 192, 193.

John Philip Kemble

Actor, 1757–1823

. . . on the 18th of the month [December 1806], at a repetition of this tragedy [*Coriolanus*], and at the very moment when Mrs. Siddons was supplicating as Volumnia, the conqueror, her son, to spare his country; when every eye should have been riveted to the scene, every ear burning with the pure flame of patriot vehemence – at such a moment an *apple* was thrown upon the stage, and fell between Mrs. Siddons and Mr. Kemble. He did not, nor would I have had him, quite dismiss the *character* he played for the *manager*, but taking up the apple, he advanced indignantly to the front of the stage, and thus addressed the audience:

LADIES AND GENTLEMEN,

I have been many years acquainted with the benevolence and liberality of a London audience; but we cannot proceed this evening with the performance unless we are protected, especially when *ladies* are thus exposed to insult.

A person in the gallery called out – 'We can't hear.'

Mr. Kemble, (*with increased spirit,*) 'I will *raise* my voice, and the GALLERIES shall *hear* me.' (*Great tumult.*)

'This protection is what the AUDIENCE owe it to themselves to *grant* – what the PERFORMERS, for the credit of their profession, have a right to *demand* – and what I will venture so far to assert, that, on the part of the PROPRIETORS, I here offer a hundred guineas to any man, who will disclose the *ruffian* who has been guilty of this act.' (A murmur, only in the gallery.)

'I throw myself, Ladies and Gentlemen, upon the high

sense of breeding, that distinguishes a London audience; and I hope I shall never be wanting in my duty to the public; but nothing shall induce me to suffer insult.'

The gallery told him that this apple of discord was thrown at some of the *disorderly females* in the boxes, and only by accident fell upon the stage. Our MORAL friends, too, sent down a request, that those *riotous ladies* might be suppressed, and Mr. Kemble good naturedly promised 'that all possible methods should be taken to keep them in order.' And then the play was finished.

James Boaden,
Memoirs of the Life of John Philip Kemble,
1825, II, 428–9.

John Kemble was notorious for his stately delivery, with marked pauses.

Kemble came to him in the evening, and they again drank very deep, and I never saw Mr. Sheridan in better spirits. Kemble was complaining of want of novelty at Drury Lane Theatre; and that, as manager, he felt uneasy at the lack of it. 'My dear Kemble,' said Mr. Sheridan, 'don't talk of grievances, now.' But Kemble still kept on saying, 'Indeed, we must seek for novelty, or the theatre will sink – novelty, and novelty alone, can prop it.'

'Then,' replied Sheridan with a smile, 'if you want novelty, act *Hamlet*, and have music played between your pauses.'

Kemble, however he might have felt the sarcasm, did not appear to take it in bad part. What made the joke tell at the time, was this: a few nights previous, while Kemble was acting Hamlet, a gentleman came to the pit door, and tendered half price. The money taker told him that the third act was only then begun.

The gentleman, looking at his watch, said, It must be impossible, for that it was half past nine o'clock.

'That is very true, Sir,' replied the money taker; 'but recollect, Mr. Kemble plays Hamlet tonight.'

Michael Kelly,
Reminiscences of Michael Kelly, 1826, pp. 342–3.

Kemble would never see Kean or any of his performances at Drury Lane at the time he was drawing all London by his extraordinary genius. Cribb, the picture-dealer of King-street, frequently pressed Kemble to give his opinion of the new star. At length, the last of the Romans did unbend. Cribb sent him a box for Drury on one of Kean's Othello nights. Anxious to hear what Kemble would say about it, he stopped him in the street, with:

'Well, you did see the little man, Kean, eh?' laughing.

'No, sir, I did not see Mr. Kean. I saw Othello; and further, I shall never act the part again.'

And with a tragedy stride, he left the delighted picture-dealer rubbing his hands in great glee.

Edmund Stirling,
Old Drury Lane, 1881, II, 148–9.

During the recurrent mental illness of George III *King Lear* was kept off the English stage, partly no doubt because theatre managements and audiences considered it bad taste to attract attention to the king's distress, but also because the Lord Chamberlain reminded theatres from time to time not to perform Shakespeare's tragedy. Whitbread wrote to the Lord Chamberlain, Lord Hertford, from Drury Lane on 28 November 1814 to assure him that *King Lear* would not be acted there, but at Covent Garden Kemble wanted to act Lear before his retirement. It was, however, 'intimated to the proprietors by the Lord Chamberlain, that it was not the wish of the Government that the play should be performed at the present time [June 1817].'

L. W. Conolly,
The Censorship of English Drama 1737–1824,
1976, p. 126.

George Frederick Cooke

Actor, 1756–1812

Cooke seems to have pretty often taken very extraordinary liberties with his audiences. Acting once [as Richard III] in Liverpool, he was hissed for being so far drunk as to render his declamation unintelligible. He turned savagely upon the people. 'What! do you hiss me! – hiss George Frederick Cooke! you contemptible money-getters! You shall never again have the honour of hissing me! Farewell! *I* banish *you*.' After a moment's pause, he added, in his deepest tones, '*There is not a brick in your dirty town but what is cemented by the blood of a negro!*'

W. Clark Russell,
Representative Actors, 1888, p. 235.

William Bensley

Actor, 1738–1817

He had to play Henry VI in 'Richard the Third.' After the monarch's death in the early part of the play, he had to appear for a moment or two as his own ghost, in the fifth act. The spirits were at that time exhibited *en buste* by a trap. Now our Henry was invited out to supper, and being anxious to get there early, and knowing that little more than his shoulders would be seen by the public, he retained his black velvet vest and bugles, but discarding the lower part of his stage costume, he drew on a jaunty pair of new, tight, nankeen pantaloons, to be as far dressed for his supper company as he could. When he stood on the trap, he cautioned the men who turned the crank not to raise him as high as usual, and of course they promised to obey. But a wicked low comedian was at hand, whose love of mischief prevailed over his judgment, and he suddenly applied himself with such good-will to the winch, that he ran King Henry up right to a level with the stage; and moreover, gave his majesty such a jerk that he was forced to step from the trap on to the boards to save himself from falling. The sight of the old Lancastrian monarch in a costume of two such different periods – mediaeval above, all nankeen and novelty below – was destructive of all decorum both before the stage and upon it. The audience emphatically 'split their sides,' and as for the tyrant in the tent, he sat bolt upright, and burst into such an insane roar that the real Richard could not have looked more frantically hysterical had the deceased Henry actually so visited him in the spirit.

Dr. [J.] Doran, *Table Traits*, quoted in W. Clark Russell, *Representative Actors*, 1888, pp. 178–9.

•

A well-loved piece of traditional business in *Hamlet* was the First Gravedigger's removal of a host of waistcoats. This practice, which emerged in the latter part of the eighteenth century, is here reported by a visitor to England: it is during a performance of *Hamlet* at Covent Garden on 20 April 1811.

After beginning their labour, and breaking ground for a grave, a conversation begins between the two grave-diggers. The chief one [Fawcett] takes off his coat, folds it carefully, and puts it by in a safe corner; then, taking up his pickaxe, spits in his hand, – gives a stroke or two, – talks, – stops, – strips off his waistcoat, still talking, – folds it with great deliberation and nicety, and puts it with the coat, – then an under-waistcoat, still talking, – another and another. I counted seven or eight, each folded or unfolded very leisurely, in a manner always different, and with gestures faithfully copied from nature. The British public enjoys this scene excessively, and the pantomimic variations a good actor knows how to introduce in it, are sure to be vehemently applauded.

Louis Simond, *Journal of a Tour and a Residence in Great Britain*, 1815, II, 121–2.

Arthur Colby Sprague, who cited this passage in *Shakespeare and the Actors* (1944), p. 175, went on to report several sightings in the twentieth century.

Mr. Allan Wilkie, early in his long career on the stage, played Second Gravedigger to the First of Alfred Tate, an actor who was known to use the old business. Mr. Wilkie confesses that he planned to play the trick on him described in Paul Bedford's *Recollections and Wanderings* – that is, to put on, surreptitiously, each waistcoat the other took off, so that as the First Gravedigger grew thinner the Second grew fatter.

But Tate gave him no chance, carefully folding each discarded waistcoat and making 'a neat pile of them well within his view.'

Arthur Colby Sprague,
The Stage Business in Shakespeare's Plays: a Postscript, 1953, p. 22.

Politics were mixed with patriotism. At a performance of *Measure for Measure* in April 1813 (the period of the 'Delicate investigation' into the conduct of Princess Caroline),

> When Lucio complained of the harshness of his sentence, being no less than 'whipping and hanging,' the Duke rejoins 'Sland'ring a *Prince* deserves it': the audience seconded the assertion by a peal of applause; upon a cessation of which some person from the gallery exclaimed – 'More so for a *Princess*!' which drew forth a volley of approbation, three times repeated.

Kathleen Barker,
The Theatre Royal Bristol 1766–1966, 1974, p. 68.
The citation is to the *Bristol Gazette*, 29 April 1813.

Solomon Franklin ('Sol') Smith

Comedian and theatre manager, 1801–1869

Sol Smith, who later became a famous actor-manager, infiltrates a performance of *Richard III* at Albany, New York, in the 1810s.

About six o'clock I entered the back door, which happened to be unguarded at the time, and went up to my old quarters in the carpenters' gallery. I felt my way in the dark until I found something which appeared to be a large box, into which I popped without the least hesitation, and closed the lid. For more than an hour I lay concealed, safe, as I thought, from discovery. At length the bustle of the carpenters and tuning of the instruments in the orchestra announced that the operations of the evening were about to commence. The curtain rose, and I ventured to peep down upon the stage. I was delighted; I could see all that was going on, myself unseen. The second act was about to begin, and I was luxuriating in the pleasure I should derive from the 'courting scene' of Richard and Lady Anne, when I heard four or five men making their way directly to my hiding-place. I had barely time to enter my box and close the lid, when I found, to my utter dismay, that the box was the object of the search; in short, as you will already have anticipated, *I was shut up in King Henry's coffin*! Here was a situation for a stage-struck hero!

The coffin was taken up, the men remarking 'it was devilish heavy,' and I felt myself conveyed down stairs and placed upon the bier. Since I had been carried so far, I made up my mind to carry the joke a little farther. So I lay as quiet as the 'injured king' would have laid had he been in my place, and was carried by four strong supernumeraries on the stage, followed by the weeping Lady Anne and all the court. Little did the lady imagine she was weeping over a living corpse! For my part I perspired most profusely, and longed for an opportunity to escape. When I was carried off 'to Whitefriars' to be interred, the supers were desired to replace the coffin in the carpenters' gallery. Being awkward (did you ever see supernumeraries who were not?), and finding their load rather heavy, they turned and tumbled it about in such a way that I could not bear it any longer, and was obliged to call out. The men dropped their precious burden and ran away in affright, which gave me an opportunity to make my escape from the coffin, and my exit through the back door.

I afterwards heard that the affair had made a great noise in the theatre at the time of its occurrence – the four men declaring that a hollow voice had issued from the coffin bidding them 'put it down and be d – d to them!' and the carpenters affirming, on the contrary, that when they opened the coffin they had found it empty. The four supernumerary gentlemen never visited the playhouse again, but immediately joined the Church. One of them, I believe, has become a notorious preacher, and never spares the theatre or theatrical people in his sermons, telling his hearers that he had a most mysterious warning when he was a young man!

Sol Smith,
Theatrical Management in the West and South for Thirty Years, New York: 1868, pp. 46–7.

Sarah Siddons

Actress, 1755–1831

Mrs Siddons as Lady Macbeth.

It was my custom to study my character at night, when all the domestic cares and business of the day were over. On the night preceding that in which I was to appear in this part for the first time, I put myself up, as usual, when all the family were retired, and commenced my study of *Lady Macbeth*. As the character is very short, I thought I should soon accomplish it. Being then only twenty years of age, I believed, as many others do believe, that little more was necessary than to get the words into my head; for the necessity of discrimination, and the development of character, at that time of my life, had scarcely entered into my imagination. But to proceed, I went on with tolerable composure, in the silence of the night (a night I can never forget), till I came to the assassination scene, when the horrors of the scene rose to a degree that made it impossible for me to get farther. I snatched up my candle, and hurried out of the room, in a paroxysm of terror. My dress was made of silk, and the rustling of it, as I ascended the stairs to go to bed, seemed to my panic-struck fancy like the movement of a spectre pursuing me. At last I reached my chamber, where I found my husband fast asleep. I clapt my candlestick down upon the table, without the power of putting the candle out; and I threw myself on my bed, without daring to stay even to take off my clothes.

Thomas Campbell,
Life of Mrs Siddons, 1834, II, 35–6.

Mrs Siddons as Volumnia.

In the second scene of the second act of *Coriolanus*, after the victory of the battle of Corioli, an ovation in honour of the victor was introduced with great and imposing effect by John Kemble. On reference to the stage directions of my father's interleaved copy, I find that no fewer than 240 persons marched in stately procession across the stage. In addition to the recognized dramatis personae (thirty-five in number), there were vestals, and lictors with their fasces, and soldiers with the spolia opima, and sword-bearers, and standard-bearers, and cup-bearers, and silver eagle-bearers with the S.P.Q.R. upon them, and trumpeters, and drummers, and priests, and dancing girls, etc., etc.

Now in this procession, and as one of the central figures in it, Mrs. Siddons had to walk. Had she been content to follow in the beaten track of her predecessors in the part, she would have marched across the stage, from right to left, with the solemn, stately, almost funeral, step conventional. But at the time, as she often did, she forgot her own identity. She was no longer Sarah Siddons, tied down to the directions of the prompter's book – or trammelled by old traditions – she was Volumnia, the proud mother of a proud son and conquering hero. So that, when it was time for her to come on, instead of dropping each foot at equi-distance in its place, with mechanical exactitude and in cadence subservient to the orchestra; deaf to the guidance of her woman's ear, but sensitive to the throbbings of her haughty mother's heart, with flashing eye, and proudest smile, and head erect, and hands pressed firmly on her bosom as if to repress by manual force its triumphant swellings, she towered above all around, and rolled and almost reeled across the stage; her very soul as it were dilating and rioting in its exultation; until her action lost all grace and yet became so true to nature, so picturesque and so descriptive, that pit and gallery sprang to their feet, electrified by the transcendent execution of an original conception.

Julian Charles Young,
A Memoir of Charles Mayne Young, Tragedian,
1871, I, 61–2.

Mrs Siddons is rescued in the nick of time.

The other night had very nearly terminated *all my exertions*, for whilst I was standing for the statue in the *Winter's Tale*, my drapery flew over the lamps that were placed behind the pedestal; it caught fire, and had it not been for one of the scene-men, who most humanely crept on his knees and extinguished it, without my knowing anything of the matter, I might have been burnt to death, or, at all events, I should have been frightened out of my senses. Surrounded as I was with muslin, the flame would have run like wildfire. The bottom of the train was entirely burned. But for the man's promptitude, it would seem as if my fate would have been inevitable. I have well rewarded the good man, and I regard my deliverance as a most gracious interposition of Providence.

Percy Fitzgerald, *The Kembles*, 1871, II, 23–4.

[Mrs Siddons] was getting significant warnings to withdraw in the shape of growing physical weakness, which should not be exhibited to an audience. Thus, when she knelt to the Duke in *Measure for Measure*, two attendants had to come forward to help her to rise; and, to save appearances, the awkward shift was resorted to of making the same ceremonial attend on the rising up of a younger actress who did not need such support.

Percy Fitzgerald, *The Kembles*, 1871, II, 146.

Mrs Siddons's last professional appearance, as Lady Macbeth.

Monday, 29 June 1812

Covent Garden Theatre I went to, it being the night on which Mrs. Siddons was to take leave of the stage . . . The House was crowded in an extraordinary manner in every part. Persons of High distinction were in the uppermost Boxes – Ladies as well as Gentlemen.

The performance of Kemble & Mrs. Siddons was most excellent. Both reminded me much of *Garrick*, notwithstanding the difference of features the expressions of their faces brought Him strongly to my mind. When Mrs. Siddons walked off the Stage in Her last scene where she appears as walking in Her sleep, there was a long continued burst of applause, which caused Kemble &c. to conclude that it was the wish of the spectators that the Play should there stop. The Curtain was dropped & much noise was continued. One of the Performers came forward to request to know whether it was the pleasure of the audience that the Play shd. stop or go on. A tumult again ensued, which being considered as a sign that the Play shd. stop, some time elapsed till at length the Curtain was drawn up and Mrs. Siddons appeared sitting at a table in Her own character. She was dressed in White Sattin, and had on a long vail. She arose but it was some-time before she could speak the clapping & other sounds of approbation rendering it impossible for Her to be Heard. She curtsied &

bowed, at last there was silence. At 10 oClock precisely she began to speak Her farewell address which took up Eight minutes during which time there was profound silence. Having finished the loudest claps &c. followed & she withdrew bowing & led off by an attendant who advanced for that purpose.

. . . Her appearance was that of a person distressed & sunk in spirits, but I did not perceive that she shed tears. J. Kemble came on afterwards to ask 'Whether the Play shd. go on?' He wiped His eyes and appeared to have been weeping. The Play was not allowed to go on.

Joseph Farington, *The Diary of Joseph Farington*, ed. Kathryn Cave, 1983, XI, 4150–1.

Robert 'Romeo' Coates

Actor, 1772–1848

'Romeo' Coates had a brief notoriety, as an amateur actor of considerable wealth and minimal talent. He starred in certain productions for which he provided the backing, and which the town came to revel in.

But there was a fresh scene, and this time of unexampled pathos, when Mr. Coates appeared at the Haymarket Theatre in *Romeo and Juliet* [1813] on the occasion of a benefit performance in aid of Miss Fitzhenry, the daughter of an old lady named Lady Perrott, who had invoked Mr. Coates' aid on a previous occasion. Miss Fitzhenry, as Juliet, became so terrified by the menacing attitude of the audience, that, shrieking, she clung to the scenery and pillars in great agitation; and could not be dislodged. Another time, in the duel scene where Romeo kills Tybalt, all was ruined, and the house was convulsed with laughter at the appearance of a bantam cock, which strutted at the very feet of Romeo, at whom it had been thrown. Mr. Coates was in despair, but luckily, at the last and darkest moment, old Capulet seized the cause of the trouble, and bore him, crowing loudly, and flapping his wings, off the stage.

. . . The play continued, though, when Romeo left the stage after killing Tybalt, he stood in the wings and shook his sword at the box from which the cock had been thrown on to the stage, with the result that the occupants of the box yelled that he must apologise for shaking his sword. Mr. Coates, very naturally, refused to do so, and the interruptions continued until the occupants of the pit turned on the interrupters and pelted them with orange peel. The play continued, then, without any further interruption until the moment came when Romeo kills Paris. Then the latter, lying dead upon the ground, was raised to life by 'a terrific blow on the nose from an orange'. The corpse rose to his feet and, pointing in a dignified way to the cause of his revival, made his way off the stage. Mr. Coates, we are told, was 'considerably annoyed' during the Tomb Scene, by shouts of 'Why don't you die?'

Edith Sitwell, *English Eccentrics*, 1957, pp. 158–60.

Edmund Kean

Actor, 1787–1833

Kean's first night as Shylock, Drury Lane, 26 January 1814.

Act III commenced, Bassanio, Antonio, and Gratiano, and, in fact, all the characters save Shylock, Tubal, Salarino, and Salanio, were quietly seated in the green-room, when the dread rumble of reiterated plaudits burst on their ears –

'Again! – again!! *What* could it be?' not '*Who* could it be?' for of that there was now no doubt. The green-room was cleared in an instant, and every character was at the wing to look at 'the little man in the *black* wig,' who was raging like a lion in the great scene with Tubal: the applause was, considering the scanty number of the audience, prodigious; as Oxberry very drolly said, 'How the devil so few of them kicked up such a row was marvellous!' At the end of this scene Kean ran up stairs to the room where he had dressed to avoid his congratulators, and in the deep recesses of his own proud heart bury his joys. It appeared to those who were unused to Kean's enunciation, that he had become hoarse from exertion, but in fact he was never in better voice. However, after him went Messrs. Raymond and Arnold, one bearing negus and the other oranges; and believe me, 'my pensive public,' the fact of those great functionaries having done this proves that the impression he had made was by no means a slight one. The trial scene (though highly applauded) was rather an anti-climax in effect: such, in fact, it always was, for his scene with Salanio and Tubal was so overwhelming, that nothing could exceed it. Shylock ends in the fourth act, and before the play was over, Kean had left the theatre.

Leman Rede, quoted in B. W. Procter (Barry Cornwall), *The Life of Edmund Kean*, 1835, II, 252–3.

I doubt if there is a more difficult character in some respects than Shylock to excel in, especially in the powerful scene where the Jew upbraids Salanio and Salarino, followed at once by the tremendous interview between Tubal and himself. The fact of rushing on the stage in a white-hot frenzy, with nothing to lead up to its gamut of passions, is the main difficulty. Of the many Shylocks I can remember, Charles Kean did most with this particular scene, his performance being, I have no doubt, as far as he could make it so, a reproduction of his father's. *A propos* of which, my wife's father has often told me, amongst many interesting stage episodes of his early career, of his having, when a country actor, played Tubal with Edmund Kean, who did not appear at rehearsal, but sent word to the theatre that 'he should like to see the gentleman who was to act the part of Tubal, at his hotel.' Mr. Wilton obeyed the summons, and dwelt always on the kindness with which Kean received and instructed him, after saying, 'We'll run through the scene, Mr. Wilton, because I am told that if you don't know, beforehand, what I'm going to do, I might frighten you!' Mr. Wilton described the performance at night as *stupendous*! and said that, although so prepared, Kean really frightened him out of his wits.

Marie and Squire Bancroft, *The Bancrofts: Recollections of Sixty Years*, 1909, pp. 209–10.

James Winston was manager of Drury Lane Theatre. His journal records several instances of Kean requiring a whore before and during the performance.

5 June 1820

On Kean being asked by Russell whether he would require to wait long between the acts [of *Richard III*], he said, 'No, not now, his *bubo* was broke' – same night a woman waiting.

17 January 1820

Kean requested the rehearsal might not be till twelve as he should get drunk that night – said he had frequently three women to stroke during performances and that two waited while the other was served. Penley said he had [formerly] seen Storace waiting for her turn. This night he had one woman (Smith) though he was much infected.

16 March 1825

Kean, about three o'clock in the morning, ordered a hackney coach to his door, took a lighted candle, got in, and rode off. He was not heard of till the Thursday noon when they found him in his room at the theatre fast asleep wrapt up in a large white greatcoat. He then sent off for a potence, some ginger, etc., and said, 'Send me Lewis or the other woman. I must have a fuck, and then I shall do.' He had it. They let him sleep till about six, when they awoke him, dressed him, and he acted but was not very sober. After the play [we] got him to supper at Sigel's lodgings and got him to a bedroom and locked him up till the morning.

Kean's agreement was signed in my room by Elliston on Thursday morning and by Kean in the evening just after he had finished playing Hamlet.

James Winston, *Drury Lane Journal: Selection from James Winston's Diaries 1819–1827*, ed. Alfred L. Nelson and Gilbert B. Cross, 1974, pp. 11, 4 and 107.

Kean cared less for delineating human nature than he did for making a point tell; and never asked what sort of a *character* he was to represent, but what sort of a *part* he was to play – not what individual he should delineate, but what effects he should produce. King Lear was to him only an admirable medium of obtaining applause, and valued in proportion to that applause. He is reported to have said (during the illness of George III, when that play was interdicted) that the public had never seen what he could do, not would they, until they saw him over the dead body of Cordelia. Yet, when the accession of George IV enabled him to appear as Lear, he was content to play it according to Nahum Tate's version. Some years afterwards, when Hazlitt's essays, and Hazlitt's advice and remonstrance had aroused him, he persuaded the Drury-lane management to restore the fifth act of Shakespeare; it was thus played a few nights, but the effect (!) was not equal to his expectations, and he relinquished Shakespeare, and resumed Tate's tragedy.

Leman Rede, quoted in B. W. Procter (Barry Cornwall), *The Life of Edmund Kean*, 1835, II, 253–4.

Small and insignificant in figure, [Kean] could at times become impressively commanding by the lion-like power and grace of his bearing. I remember, the last time I saw him play Othello, how puny he appeared beside Macready, until in the third act, when roused by Iago's taunts and insinuations, he moved towards him with a gouty hobble, seized him by the throat, and, in a well-known explosion, 'Villain! be sure you prove,' etc., seemed to swell into a stature which made Macready appear small. On that very evening, when gout made it difficult for him to display his accustomed grace, when a drunken hoarseness had ruined the once matchless voice, such was the irresistible pathos – manly, not tearful – which vibrated in his tones and expressed itself in look and gestures, that old men leaned their heads upon their arms and fairly sobbed.

George Henry Lewes,
On Actors and the Art of Acting, 1875, pp. 15–16.

At a time when some of the public prints were jesting as to his infirmities (supposing them to be fictitious), we ourselves can testify to their reality. It must have been nearly two years previous to his death, when we went behind the scenes of Covent Garden Theatre. He was playing Richard the Third. No one, in *front* of the curtain, perceived any diminution in his vigour. But behind! There was the last of the Plantagenets, sitting at one of the side-scenes, panting, flushed, and bent almost double by exhaustion. A servant stood by his chair, with a goblet of brandy-and-water (evidently *very* strong) in his hand. It had lost some of its heat, and the tragedian impatiently ordered another to be brought, 'stronger, and very hot.' In a minute afterwards, the call-boy required his presence on the stage, and there he was accordingly, apparently as vigorous and active as ever, and bringing down from boxes and galleries repeated acclamations. The scene terminated, and we saw him again a drooping, panting and exhausted man.

B.W. Procter (Barry Cornwall),
The Life of Edmund Kean, 1835, II, 236–7.

Kean's last performances.

Now and then the town saw him, but his hold on it was nearly gone. He was now at the Haymarket; and then, uncertainly, at Drury Lane; and again at the Haymarket in 1832, where I saw him for the last of many times, in Richard. The sight was pitiable. Genius was not traceable in that bloated face; intellect was all but quenched in those once matchless eyes; and the power seemed gone, despite the will that would recall it. I noted in a diary, that night, the above facts, and, in addition, that by bursts he was as grand as he had ever been, – that though he looked well as long as he was still, he moved only with difficulty, using his sword as a stick . . . but he was exhausted before the fifth act, and when, after a short fight, Richmond (Cooper) gave him his death-wound in Bosworth Field, as he seemed to deal the blow, he grasped Kean by the hand, and let him gently down, lest he should be injured by a fall.

. . . He aroused himself to make his last appearance, as it proved, on the stage, in conjunction with his son, in Othello, Mr. Charles Kean playing Iago. The night was the 25th of March 1833. Edmund Kean was so shattered in frame, that he had scarcely strength to pass over him the dress of the Moor; so shattered in nerve, that he dreaded some disaster. Brandy gave some little heart to the greatly fallen actor, but he anxiously enjoined his son to be ever near him, in case of some mischance, and he went through the part, dying as he went, till after giving the sweet utterance, as of old, to the celebrated 'Farewell,' ending with 'Othello's occupation's gone!' he attempted to utter the next speech, and in the attempt fell on his son's shoulder, with a whispered moan, 'I am dying, – speak to them for me!' The curtain here descended on him for ever, and the rest was only slow death, with intervals of hope.

Dr [J.] Doran, *Annals of the English Stage from Thomas Betterton to Edmund Kean*, ed. Robert Lowe, 1888, III, 412–15.

Charles Kemble

Actor, 1775–1854

Charles Kemble's production of *King John* at Covent Garden, 1823, ushered in the era of scrupulous accuracy in matters of costume and historical detail. J. R. Planché was in charge of the preparations for the play.

Never shall I forget the dismay of some of the performers when they looked upon the flat-topped *chapeaux de fer (fer blanc*, I confess) of the 12th Century, which they irreverently called *stewpans*! Nothing but the fact that the classic features of a Kemble were to be surrounded by a precisely similar abomination would, I think, have induced one of the rebellious barons to have appeared in it. They had no faith in me, and sulkily assumed their new and strange habiliments, in the full belief that they would be roared at by the audience. They *were* roared at; but in a much more agreeable way than they had contemplated. When the curtain rose, and discovered King John dressed as his effigy appears in Worcester Cathedral, surrounded by his barons sheathed in mail, with cylindrical helmets and correct armorial shields, and his courtiers in the long tunics and mantles of the thirteenth century, there was a roar of applause, so generous and hearty, that the actors were astonished, and I felt amply rewarded for all the trouble, anxiety, and annoyance I had experienced during my labours. Receipts of from 400*l.* to 600*l.* nightly soon reimbursed the management for the expense of the production, and a complete reformation of dramatic costume became from that moment inevitable upon the English stage.

J. R. Planché,
Recollections and Reflections, 1872, I, 56–7.

Robert William Elliston

Actor, 1774–1831

Those who have imagined that an unexpected elevation to the direction of a great London theatre affected the consequence of Elliston, or at all changed his nature, knew not the essential *greatness* of the man whom they disparage. It was my fortune to encounter him near St Dunstan's Church (which, with its punctual giants, is now no more than dust and a shadow), on the morning of his election to that high office. Grasping my hand, with a look of significance, he only uttered, 'Have you heard the news?' Then, with another look following up the blow, he subjoined, 'I am the future manager of Drury Lane Theatre.' Breathless as he saw me, he stayed not for congratulation or reply, but mutely stalked away, leaving me to chew upon his new-blown dignities at leisure. In fact, nothing could be said to it. Expressive silence alone could muse his praise. This was in his *great* style.

But was he less *great* . . . when, in melancholy after-years, again, much near the same spot, I met him when that sceptre had been wrested from his hand, and his dominion was curtailed to the petty managership and part proprietorship of the small Olympic, *his Elba*? He still played nightly upon the boards of Drury, but in parts, alas! allotted to him, not magnificently sinking the sense of fallen *material* grandeur in the more liberal resentment of depreciations done to his more lofty *intellectual* pretensions. 'Have you heard' (his customary exordium) – 'have you heard', said he, 'how they treat me? They put me in *comedy*.' Thought I – but his finger on his lips forbade any verbal interruption – 'Where could they have put you better?' Then, after a pause – 'Where I formerly played Romeo, I now play Mercutio'; and so again he stalked away, neither staying nor caring for responses.

Charles Lamb, 'Ellistoniana',
The Englishman's Magazine, August 1831.

It was during Elliston's last season at Birmingham that he met Mr. Howard Payne, the 'American Roscius', with whom formerly he had had some intimacy. Elliston at this time, greatly pressed by a variety of undertakings, was advertised for playing the part of Richard III on a certain ensuing Wednesday, and was, in fact, on his way to the rehearsal, when he encountered his friend Howard Payne. After a hasty salutation and some professional inquiries, Elliston suddenly observed to his companion –

'My dear Payne, I well know your readiness in conferring favours, and, in the present instance, you are the only man in this town who could oblige me.'

'Ay! – what is it?' demanded the other.

'I am on my way to the theatre: we have a rehearsal – *Richard III*. A rehearsal must be had for the sake of my company, who are a little wild in the play. You know not, my dear fellow, the whirl in which I am at this moment – country theatres in a state of insurrection, and no solid loyalty at home. Look at these letters – must be replied to by today's post. Payne, oblige me – run to the theatre – go through the rehearsal with my people – you know the business – better, no man in the two hemispheres – set them right – put them to their work, and relieve me from this morning's annoyance.'

'Why, 'tis so long since I played the part, that really –'

'No man living could have presented himself more capable of serving me than you. The business – you know it as well as I do – come, my good fellow, run over the words as quickly as you like – only put 'em right for Wednesday night. Show them how they flog us at New York,' added he, with one of his slyest twinkles.

After a little further expostulation, on the one hand, and amicable contention on the other, Howard Payne consented, and away they went, arm in arm, to the theatre.

On entering the stage, Elliston introduced his friend to the principals in attendance, and bidding the prompter immediately call the rehearsal, once again whispered 'New York' into Howard's ear, and vanished.

Elliston's plea of business might really have been a fair one, but the machinery of his mind was of that complex nature, that no common observer could hope to understand the manufacture which was going on within. The manager now took the opportunity of gliding into the front of the theatre, where, placing himself in an obscure corner, he noticed all that was in progress on the stage. Having witnessed the very able manner in which his friend was conducting the rehearsal in one or two scenes, Elliston left the house with extreme precipitation, and, making the best of his way to his printers', set the operators there immediately to work on striking off two or three hundred bills, of an extraordinary size, announcing 'The arrival of the Celebrated American Roscius, Mr. Howard Payne, who would have the honour of appearing, on the following evening, in the part of *Richard III.*'

These bills were printed, and nearly posted, in various parts of the town before the termination of the said rehearsal; and when, at about three o'clock, the actors were retiring from their morning's task, and with them, of course, Howard Payne himself, their eyes were saluted, at the corner of almost every street, with the 'American Roscius for the following evening!' Payne, naturally enough, was thunderstruck – he then became furious; refusing, of course, to play a part into which he had been thoroughly entrapped, and went directly in search of the tricking manager. Arriving at Elliston's lodgings, he there learnt that unexpected business had called the manager suddenly away to Leicester, but that he should certainly be in Birmingham again on Wednesday night.

Furious and bewildered, poor Payne now retraced his way to the theatre, where, at every step, 'The American Roscius,' in *Niagara* type, assailed his gaze. The actors now gathered about him – Elliston was, to all intents and purposes, gone, and should Payne still refuse to act, the theatre, on the following night, would be closed, and all parties lose a night's salary. Payne who had but lately arrived in England, with the determination of following his profession, knew that he had the public to conciliate; and it was now forcibly represented to him, that should he fail to perform, the Birmingham people would, naturally enough, suspect Payne of some breach of contract with Elliston, and thus look coldly on him for the future.

The whole company therefore, with one common effort, entreated him to play the part, pleading their necessities, and professing their gratitude. Their prayers and other considerations finally prevailed. Payne consented – the morrow arrived – 'the American Roscius' was flattered by crowded boxes and pit – the actor was highly applauded – the receipts great – and Elliston, true to the Wednesday, returned to Birmingham, when all grievances were forgotten in the triumphant result of *Richard III*.

George Raymond,
Memoirs of Robert William Elliston, 1846, II, 188–91.

•

Heinrich Heine sees *The Merchant of Venice* in London.

When I saw this piece played in Drury Lane there stood behind me in the box a pale British beauty who, at the end of the fourth Act, wept passionately, and many times cried out 'The poor man is wronged!' It was a countenance of noblest Grecian cut, and the eyes were large and black. I have never been able to forget them, those great black eyes which wept for Shylock!

Heinrich Heine, *Shakespeare's Mädchen und Frauen*, 1839, translated by C. G. Leland, 1891.

Edwin Forrest

Actor, 1806–1872

In 1836 he was seen for the first time as Lear, which many critics considered his finest part. Forrest was of the same opinion himself. His magnificent physique, rugged exterior, tempestuous style of acting, all lent verisimilitude to the kingly role. A friend once remarked to him: 'Mr Forrest, I never saw you play Lear as well as you did last night.' Whereupon the actor drew himself up to his full height, and replied indignantly: '*Play* Lear! What do you mean, sir? I do not *play* Lear! I *play* Hamlet, Richard, Shylock, Virginius, but by God, sir, I *am* Lear!'

Arthur Hornblow, *A History of the Theatre in America*, Philadelphia, 1919, II, 36.

William Charles Macready

Actor, 1793–1873

The eminent tragedian opened in *Lear*; our property-man received his plot for the play in the usual manner, a map being required among the many articles (map highly necessary for Lear to divide his kingdom). The property-man being illiterate, read 'mop' for '*map*'. At night the tragedy commences; Macready in full state on his throne calls for his map, a 'super' noble, kneeling, presents the aging king a white curly mop. The astounded actor rushed off the stage, dragging the unfortunate nobleman and his mop with him, actors and audience wild with delight.

Edmund Stirling, *Old Drury Lane*, 1881, I, 119–20.

Macready's *Henry V*, 1839, was distinguished for its scenic magnificence and effects that seem now like the cinema in embryo. The English fleet was seen leaving Southampton through a moving diorama, and the siege of Harfleur took place against a painted backcloth; 'a little smoke was made to obscure the stage, and by a pantomime-trick process, the troops painted, as if in the distance, were converted into the same troops engaging'. But the reviewer in *John Bull* (17 June 1839) took up an adverse position, one destined to be popular among critics for most of a century to come.

So far has this rage for over-embellishing his author led Mr Macready that at the conclusion of the fourth act, which ends with these words, spoken by King Henry –

Do we all holy rites;
Let there be sung *Non nobis* and *Te Deum*, etc.

the actor literally kneels down with his soldiery, and the curtain falls to the solemn strains of an organ, brought from England we suppose for the purpose . . .

George C. D. Odell,
Shakespeare From Betterton To Irving, 1921, II, 222.

This is an early, perhaps the first instance of sound effects being used to create a mood outside the immediate context.

In the revival of *King John* in 1841, Macready introduced a new effect. After the fight in the third act, which results in an English victory, a part of the English force crossed the stage, preceded by trumpeters, who sounded notes of melancholy and wailing. One night, at Macready's house, Mr. W. J. Fox objected that sounds of this kind could not with propriety have proceeded from the triumphant English, the retreat alluded to in the stage directions being clearly that of the French. Macready answered that the purpose of these notes was to prepare the house for King John's sinister interview with Hubert which immediately followed. On being asked for my opinion – that of a very young man – by two who were greatly my seniors, I was diplomatic enough to observe that the question seemed to be how far a dramatic effect, finely suggestive, might be purchased at the expense of probability.

Westland Marston,
Our Recent Actors, 1890, p. 66.

In the great scene of the third act of *The Merchant of Venice*, Shylock has to come on in a state of intense rage and grief at the flight of his daughter. Now it is obviously a great trial for the actor to 'strike twelve at once.' He is one moment calm in the green-room, and the next he has to appear on the stage with his whole nature in an uproar. Unless he has a very mobile temperament, quick as flame, he cannot begin this scene at the proper state of white heat. Accordingly, we see actors in general come bawling and gesticulating, but leaving us unmoved because they are not moved themselves. Macready, it is said, used to spend some minutes behind the scenes, lashing himself into an imaginative rage by cursing *sotto voce*, and shaking violently a ladder fixed against the wall. To bystanders the effect must have been ludicrous. But to the audience the actor presented himself as one really agitated. He had worked himself up to the proper pitch of excitement which would enable him to express the rage of Shylock.

George Henry Lewes,
On Actors and the Art of Acting, 1875, p. 44.

Cincinnati, April 2nd 1849

Acted Hamlet to a rather rickety audience, but I tried my utmost, and engaged the attention of at least the greater part of the auditory. In the scene after the play with Rosencrantz and Guildenstern an occurrence took place that, for disgusting brutality, indecent outrage, and malevolent barbarism, must be without parallel in the theatre of any civilized community. Whilst speaking to them about 'the pipe,' a ruffian from the left side gallery threw into the middle of the stage the half of the raw carcase of a sheep!

The Diaries of William Charles Macready 1833–1851, ed. William Toynbee, 1912, II, 420.

•

1851. *August* 30. – The discriminating Mr Barnum has had reason to think that the English taste turns very much upon small things; and he now challenges for two miniature actors the success that attended his Tom Thumb. The 'Bateman children' are little girls respectively of eight and six, who are both pretty and clever, but whose appearance in an act of *Richard the Third* (at the ST. JAMES'S THEATRE) is a nuisance by no means proportioned to the size of its perpetrators. No doubt there is talent shown in it; and it is curious to hear such small imps of the nursery speak so fluently, and, strutting about easily, repeat a well-taught lesson with such wonderful aptitude. But this is the feeling of a moment, and nothing is left but the wearisome absurdity of such big words in such little mouths.

Henry Morley,
The Journal of a London Playgoer, 1891, p. 27.

Lester Wallack

Actor and playwright, 1820–1888

It was thought an extraordinary thing when Garrick first put on a pair of Elizabethan trunks for *Richard III*. He played Macbeth in a squarecut scarlet coat, the costume of an English general, and a regulation wig with a pigtail of his own period, while Mrs. Pritchard, who played Lady Macbeth wore an enormous hoop. Garrick desired very much to wear a Scotch tartan and kilt, and a plaid, with bare legs, the traditional Highland costume. But this was in the days of the Pretender, when no one was allowed to show a plaid in the streets of London. After Garrick had brought in a great deal of wise reform in the way of dress there was a lull again, and no one dared to do anything new. Many generations later my father was cast for the part of Tressel, in Cibber's version of *Richard III*. Tressel is the youthful messenger who conveys to King Henry VI the news of the murder of his son after the battle of Tewkesbury. My father, a young, ambitious actor, came on with the feather hanging from his cap, all wet, his hair dishevelled, one boot torn nearly off, one spur broken, the other gone entirely, his gauntlet stained with blood, and his sword snapped in twain; at which old Wewitzer, who was the manager, and had been a manager before my father was born, was perfectly shocked. It was too late to do anything then, but the next morning Wewitzer sent for him to come to his office, and addressed him thus: 'Young man, how do you ever hope to get on in your profession by deliberately breaking all precedent? What will become of the profession if mere boys are allowed to take these liberties? Why, sir, you should have entered in a suit of decent black, with silk stockings on and with a white handkerchief in your hand.'

'What! after defeat and flight from battle?' interrupted my father. 'That has nothing at all to do with it,' was the reply; 'the proprieties! Sir, the proprieties!'

Lester Wallack,
Memories of Fifty Years, 1889, pp. 175–7.

Ellen Terry

Actress, 1848–1928

Ellen Terry was a notable child actress, playing Mamillius at the age of eight in Charles Kean's production of *The Winter's Tale* at the Princess Theatre, 1856. This was the first leg of a remarkable double for she played Hermione in Beerbohm Tree's production at His Majesty's Theatre fifty years later. She here describes a mishap as Puck, in Charles Kean's *A Midsummer Night's Dream*, Princess Theatre, 1856.

It is argued now that stage life is bad for a young child, and children are not allowed by law to go on the stage until they are ten years old – quite a mature age in my young days! I cannot discuss the whole question here, and must content myself with saying that during my three years at the Princess's I was a very strong, happy, and healthy child. I was never out of the bill except during the run of *A Midsummer Night's Dream*, when, through an unfortunate accident, I broke my toe. I was playing Puck, my second part on any stage, and had come up through a trap at the end of the last act to give the final speech. My sister Kate was playing Titania that night as understudy to Carlotta Leclerq. Up I came – but not quite up, for the man shut the trap-door too soon and caught my toe. I screamed. Kate rushed to me and banged her foot on the stage, but the man only closed the trap tighter, mistaking the signal.

'Oh, Katie! Katie!' I cried. 'Oh, Nelly! Nelly!' said poor Kate helplessly. Then Mrs. Kean came rushing on and made them open the trap and release my poor foot.

'Finish the play, dear,' she whispered excitedly, 'and I'll double your salary!' There was Kate holding me up on one side and Mrs. Kean on the other. Well, I did finish the play in a fashion. The text ran something like this –

> 'If we shadows have offended (oh, Katie, Katie!)
> Think but this, and all is mended, (Oh, my toe!)
> That you have but slumbered here,
> While these visions did appear. (I can't, I can't!)
> And this weak and idle theme,
> No more yielding but a dream, (Oh, dear! oh, dear!)
> Gentles, do not reprehend; (a big sob)
> If you pardon, we will mend. (Oh, Mrs. Kean!)

How I got through it, I don't know! But my salary was doubled – it had been fifteen shillings, and it was raised to thirty – and Mr. Skey, President of St. Bartholomew's Hospital, who chanced to be in a stall that very evening, came round behind the scenes and put my toe right. He remained my friend for life.

Ellen Terry, *The Story of my Life*, 1908, pp. 16–17.

•

Ellen Terry plays Desdemona to Edwin Booth's Othello, Lyceum Theatre, 1881. Irving and Booth alternated as Othello and Iago.

At rehearsal he [Booth] was very gentle and apathetic. Accustomed to playing Othello with stock companies, he had few suggestions to make about the stage-management. The part to him was more or less of a monologue.

'I shall never make you black,' he said one morning.

'When I take your hand I shall have a corner of my drapery in my hand. That will protect you.'

I am bound to say I thought of Mr. Booth's 'protection' with some yearning the next week when I played Desdemona to *Henry's* Othello. Before he had done with me I was nearly as black as he.

Ellen Terry, *The Story of my Life*, 1908, p. 204.

Charles Kean

Actor-manager, 1811–1868

Charles Kean was the first of the Shakespearian pageant masters. He employed an army of supers, a troupe of dancers, a company of singers, a large orchestra and a host of 'machinists'. One of the busiest moments of these machinists must have been at the end of the third act of *Macbeth*, where the instructions in Kean's prompt book are: 'Hecate ascends into the air, the witches disappear, then the mist disperses and discovers A Bird's Eye View of the Island of Iona.'

Norman Marshall,
The Producer and the Play, 1975, p. 132

The carpenters of country theatres always dreaded Charles Kean's advent among them, for, in his earlier days on the stage, when he rehearsed, he would steadily go through his own scenes just as at night. During this time silence was strictly ordered to be observed all over the theatre; a creaking boot, a cough, a sneeze, the knocking of a hammer, would distress the tragedian beyond measure. It was on pain of dismissal that any carpenter or other servant caused the smallest interruption during Mr. Kean's scenes. This naturally caused much ill-humour amongst the men, and when it became known by the carpenters that 'Kean was coming,' there would be various expressions of discontent. At the commencement of one particular engagement these men formed a conspiracy amongst themselves. The opening play was *Hamlet*, and they conceived a plot by which the Royal Dane might be induced to 'cut short' his long soliloquies. One particular man was to place himself at the back of the gallery, being quite hidden from sight, and just as Kean began his great soliloquy was to call out in a muffled voice to an imaginary fellow-workman. This was the result:

KEAN (in slow, measured tones): To be or *not* to be (long pause) – that is the question.

VOICE (far-off in front of house, calling): Jo Attwood!

KEAN (stopping and looking in the direction, then commencing again): To be – or *not* – to – be – that is the question.

VOICE: Jo Attwood!

KEAN (bewildered and annoyed): Will somebody find Mr. Attwood? (A pause.) To be or *not* to be – that is the question.

VOICE: Jo Attwood!

KEAN: Until Mr. Attwood is found I cannot go on!

'Mr. Attwood' could *not* be found, and the voice did not cease interrupting Kean, who, at last, gave up his attempt to rehearse and went home; upon which the carpenters rejoiced in a sort of triumphant war-dance.

Marie and Squire Bancroft, *The Bancrofts: Recollections of Sixty Years*, 1909, pp. 42–3.

Mrs. Charles Kean inherited to the full the traditions of the great Sarah Siddons, and several good stories are related of her tragic manner in private life. One such is too good to be omitted.

A young actor had discovered that his black tights for the part of Horatio had not arrived, and he was obliged to put on red ones. After the show, he called to see Mr. Kean to explain matters. The door was opened by Mrs. Kean. 'What do you want, sir?' 'To see Mr. Charles Kean.' Mrs. Kean makes a stately and dramatic exit. She returns imploring silence with dramatic gestures. 'What might your business be?' she solemnly asks. Horatio explains that he wishes to apologize for his red tights. 'Would Mr. Kean forgive him?' Mrs. Kean exits again solemnly and returns with a more seraphic countenance. 'Mr. Kean will pardon you; but (pointing ecstatically to heaven), will you be forgiven *there*?' It is also said of her that in the part of Queen Katherine she was especially terrifying in her gestures, and that the denunciatory finger held up to Cardinal Wolsey was more suggestive of 'No pudding for you to-day, my boy,' than anything else.

Erroll Sherson,
London's Lost Theatres of the Nineteenth Century,
1925, pp. 135–6.

•

The first horseback version of *Richard III* in England was seen in 1856.

. . . Astley's amphitheatre in 1856 was filled almost nightly for months with an equestrian extravaganza featuring White Surrey and his heroic exploits on the field of battle. The playbills, about two-and-a-half feet long, announce in black and red and numerous different type faces that 'riderless steeds gallop to and fro over the Plain; the gallant charger "White Surrey", while bearing his Royal master, Falls dead in the field – the stage is covered with DYING AND DEAD HORSES while the Tout Ensemble produces an effect such as never yet has been attempted by any Stud of Horses in the World – the whole forming a Grand and Startling Representation.' As one paper put it, 'whenever the text makes allusion to horses, horses illustrate the text.'

Julie Hankey, *Plays in Performance: Richard III*,
second edition, 1981, p. 58.

John Coleman

Actor, 18?? – 1904

Coleman offends mid-century ideas of playing Richard III.

At that time the popular Cibberian idea of the last of the Plantagenets was the monster indubitably designed by the Bard (who, I fear, was a bit of a courtier) to incarnate the mass of lies and libels handed down to posterity by the venal hirelings of the Tudor adventurer, who murdered (see Polydore Virgil) his noble adversary at Bosworth, and mangled and defiled the hero's body afterwards. As a literary work I admit that I was bound to carry out the author's idea, but the brutal vulgarity of this scowling, gibbering ruffian jarred upon me, and I elected to take Bulwer's view of the subject, making my Richard what the Countess of Desmond described him to be – a courtly, elegant gentleman, slightly round-shouldered. Grunt and grimace, bandy-legs and cork-screw ringlets I discarded altogether. I wore my own hair – I had plenty of it in those days. The pit and boxes endured me with placid severity; but the Olympians missed their beloved Quilp and *Quasimodo* monstrosity. The king of the gallery indignantly enquired, 'Where's your 'ump? You ain't got no 'ump. The idea of King Dick without a 'ump!'

The old stagers were all opposed to my innovations. 'The old style was good enough for Kean,' they said, 'and ought to be good enough for you. The idea of a raw, inexperienced boy daring to discard the glorious traditions of the past! What next?'

My King Henry, 'Romeo' Maddocks (so called from having acted Romeo with dubious success with Emmeline

Montague before the Queen at Covent Garden) delivered himself anent my unfortunate performance in this oracular fashion, 'My good young friend, your Richard is all a mistake! You haven't the most distant idea of the part. You should see *me* in it! I've all Edmund Kean's business. Ah, sir, the little man was wonderful! You make nothing of *my* death. When he killed me and said, 'Down – down to hell, and say I sent thee thither!' he threw his great moons of eyes up to the gallery, and down came three tremendous rounds of applause!'

'But why on earth did he throw his eyes up to heaven when he was sending Henry down to hell?'

'Why – why? Because he chose to do so, and whatever the divine Edmund chose to do was right!'

John Coleman,
Fifty Years of an Actor's Life, 1904, II, 466–8.

•

In 1858, Harley, while playing Bottom, was seized by paralysis and died in a few hours, his last strange words being from his part, 'I have an exposition of sleep come upon me.'

Percy Fitzgerald,
A New History of the English Stage, 1882, II, 346.

Sir Henry Irving

Actor-manager, 1838–1905

One night at supper in the Beefsteak Room, Irving told me an amusing occurrence which took place at Manchester when Booth played there. He said it was 'about' 1863, so it may have been that time of which I have written – 1861. *Richard III* was put up, Charles Calvert, the manager, playing

Richmond, and Booth Gloster. Calvert determined to make a brave show of his array against the usurper, and being manager was able to dress his own following to some measure of his wishes. Accordingly he drained the armoury of the theatre and had the armour furbished up to look smart. Richard's army came on in the usual style. They were not much to look at though they were fairly comfortable for their work of fighting. But Richmond's army enthralled the sense of the spectators, till those who knew the play began to wonder how such an army *could* be beaten by the starvelings opposed to them. They were not used to fight, or even to move in armour, however; and the moment they began to make an effort they one and all fell down and wriggled all over the stage in every phase of humiliating but unsuccessful effort to get up; and the curtain had to be lowered amidst the wild laughter of the audience.

Bram Stoker,
Personal Reminiscences of Henry Irving, 1907, p. 58.

Henry Irving plays *Hamlet* with a largely amateur cast in Bury, Lancashire, 1865.

Some curious incidents happened. I recollect I played Polonius (wearing a beard which I would *not* cut off); it was thought that my flowing fur-trimmed robe would go well with the hirsute appendage. My arms were bare, and altogether I must have looked very barbaric. Amateur-like, I burst out laughing when Irving said in a very pointed manner, and a merry twinkle in his eye, '*You* to the barber's with your beard.' I remember the weather was very hot, and after being consigned to oblivion, I was sitting on a table behind the tapestry, fanning myself, when, to my astonishment, Hamlet drew aside the tapestry, and repeating the well-known words, 'Thou wretched, rash, intruding fool, farewell. I took thee for thy better', he gave me an agonized look, and *sotto voce* exclaimed: 'For goodness' sake get me a pint of stout!

I'm as dry as a limekiln.' This, from the Prince of Denmark, startled me, and for some little time I failed to take in the situation.

Alfred Darbyshire,
The Art of the Victorian Stage, 1907, p. 88.

At rehearsals he would waste no time – but we often wasted it for him. I remember that an actor who was to play *Kent* in *King Lear*, wasted about an hour at one of the rehearsals in the vain attempt to make the gesture of tripping someone up with his foot – to make this at the right moment, on the right syllable of the right word. The line was: '*Nor tripped neither you base football player*,' and the actor made sundry jabs with first one foot and then the other, always on the wrong word. Irving held that there was a right word on which to do it, while this actor, unconscious that such a thing as the right word existed, would try it first on the word '*nor*,' then on the word '*tripped*,' or after the word '*neither*,' or on the word '*base*' – and finally on the first syllable of the word '*player*.' On these words he would make a rough jab with his foot. What Irving was telling him to do, was to make a very slight motion, brushing the ground with his right foot (chiefly the toe part of the said foot) on the first syllable of the word '*neither*,' and on no other syllable – no other word. Over and over we went – 'Nor tripped *nei*ther' etc., and not once did he get it right . . .

I happened to be playing the part of Oswald, the one to be tripped, and so I was there all the time – luckily doing my bit rather well – and helping to the best of my ability.

'Try it again, my boy,' says the voice of the Chief to the player of Kent; and he tried it, and down I went, rather neatly for me (for I had done it by then some thirty times within forty-five minutes). We had to pretend to trip and pretend to be tripped – to act it – and the actor of *Kent* simply couldn't see why he should come swish with his foot on the word '*neither*' – on its first syllable. He got it at last – rather roughly put a kind of swing to his foot, somewhere near the right moment. What this illustrates I'm not quite sure. It could serve to show how patient Irving was – how concerned about a trifle – how passionately fond of rhythm – how dull the actor – or how obstinate – or how paralysed.

Gordon Craig, *Henry Irving*, 1930, pp. 107–9.

Henry Irving's Shylock dress was designed by Sir John Gilbert. It was never replaced, and only once cleaned by Henry's dresser and valet, Walter Collinson. Walter, I think, replaced 'Doody,' Henry's first dresser at the Lyceum, during the run of *The Merchant of Venice*. Walter was a wig-maker by trade – assistant to Clarkson the elder. It was Doody who, on being asked his opinion of a production, said that it was fine – 'not a join to be seen anywhere!' It was Walter who was asked by Henry to say which he thought his master's best part. Walter could not be 'drawn' for a long time. At last he said Macbeth.

This pleased Henry immensely, for, as I hope to show later on, he fancied himself in Macbeth more than in any other part.

'It is generally conceded to be Hamlet,' said Henry.

'Oh, no, Sir,' said Walter, '*Macbeth*. You sweat twice as much in that.'

Ellen Terry, *The Story of my Life*,
1908, pp. 182–3.

In this same play, *King Lear*, I had received from stage-manager Irving, the key to the character of *Oswald*, as I was to play it . . . It was the first rehearsal. 'Well, my boy,' he said – only he said, 'Welllll, my buy,' which was a hundred times better, of course, being proper old English – but I will translate as I go along. 'Well, my boy,' said Irving to me, as he passed me and stopped –' err – m – er – this – er – part (pat, he said) this pat – er – m, what do you – er – make of it?' All I could do was to murmur and suggest that the part seemed to me to be 'barbaric' – at which he gave an almost imperceptible leap in the air, and quietly went on, 'Yes – barbaric – barbaric – yes – err,' and by this time he was warming up – pinched his nose very slightly at the nostril – stopped dead – was about to move off – riveted me with the kindest of stern glances, and said simply 'Malvolio' – and on he passed.

With *that* in my pocket I knew what to do, and didn't hesitate. He helped me just as he would help himself – to escape from the terrible uncertainty that Shakespeare gets us into about so many of his minor characters, and to raise a small unimportant part to a role of the first magnitude – by simplifying.

Gordon Craig, *Henry Irving*, 1930, pp. 109–10.

Irving has often been gibed at for cutting the whole of the last act of *The Merchant of Venice* when he toured the play because Shylock does not appear in this act, but I have been told by an actor who was in Irving's company that this was only done because the provincial audiences were restless and inattentive during the final act. They were merely waiting for the moment when Irving would appear to take his curtain calls.

Norman Marshall,
The Producer and the Play, 1975, pp. 133–4.

He [Irving] had been taken to task, by a writer of no importance, in regard to the robe which he wore as Cardinal Wolsey. In reference to that reproach, he said: 'I had a respectful desire to represent the Cardinal in his habit as he lived, and his habits were most expensive . . . Now, a friend of mine possessed an old cardinal robe of just the colour that Wolsey wore, and I sent my robe to Rome to be dyed like that; but the old tint was no longer used there, and I had it reproduced in London. If I am told this was a prodigal caprice, I reply that it was quite in keeping with Wolsey's taste. When you are getting into the skin of a character, you need not neglect his wardrobe.'

Austin Brereton,
The Life of Henry Irving, 1908, II, 166–7.

Irving's attention to detail extended, of course, to the scenic side. Absolute accuracy was an ideal from which he never knowingly swerved. One of the scenes in *Coriolanus* showed a fishmonger's shop in a Roman thoroughfare. Anxious to achieve the necessary degree of realism, I painted outside the shop a life-like representation of a turbot. The scene, it must be understood, had to be shown twice in the play – once in the opening stages, and again towards the final fall of the curtain.

Irving was down on the turbot as soon as he set eyes on it.

'Take that fish out, my boy!' was his command. 'I'm going to the wars in the play, *and it won't keep till I get back*.'

Joseph Harker, *Studio and Stage*, 1924, pp. 127–8.

Gladstone sees *King Lear* (1892).

One other incident of the run of *King Lear* is, I think, worthy of record, inasmuch as it bears on the character and feeling of that great Englishman, Mr. Gladstone. In the second week of the run he came to see the play, occupying his usual seat on the stage on the O.P. [Opposite Prompt] corner. He seemed most interested in all that went on, but not entirely happy. At the end, after many compliments to Mr. Irving and Miss Terry, he commented on the unpatriotic conduct of taking aid from the French – from any foreigner – under any circumstances whatever of domestic stress.

Bram Stoker,
Personal Reminiscences of Henry Irving, 1907, p. 79.

'No man can stand the strain of Hamlet,' explained Sir Henry [Irving] to me, 'unless he begins playing it before the age of thirty-five.' Certainly, I should say, no part in all the range of drama makes so severe and protracted a demand upon the nervous energies. Indeed, I remember that after my first performance of the part, I arose next morning as one who had come through a long illness. And, indeed, the pain and labour of giving life to such a creation has, perhaps, no analogy so closely akin to it as that of childbirth. Nor is it only a question of the exhaustion of energy; there is an exhaustion of spirit so great that, during the long run of Hamlet at the old Lyceum, it was told me by one who was in those days his nearest and dearest friend, that Sir Henry deliberately eschewed all social distractions and allowed nothing to ruffle the calm and serene poise of his soul.

Sir John Martin-Harvey,
'Some Reflections on Hamlet',
Transactions of the Royal Society of Literature, 1916.

Tommaso Salvini

Actor, 1830–1915

Salvini's *Othello*, played in Italian, took London by storm in 1875.

As depicted in Salvini's portrayal, those passions, lying deep and dormant and scarcely known to the Moor himself, but gradually roused by guilt and fed by suspicion, carried the tragic hero relentlessly to his doom in a denouement of wild destruction that shocked critics and audiences alike in its uncompromising barbarity: Desdemona was seized by her hair, dragged to the bed and strangled with 'a ferocity that seems to take delight in its office'; Othello slashed his own throat with a scimitar, 'hacking and hewing at the flesh, severing all the cords, pipes and ligatures that there meet, and making the hideous noises that escaping air and bubbling blood are likely to produce.' It is said that strong men in the audience blanched and women fainted; but the acting profession called for a special morning matinee and Irving, unable to attend that, crept in to a later performance, describing it as 'a thing to wonder at'.

Kenneth Richards, 'Shakespeare and the Italian Players in Victorian London',
Shakespeare and the Victorian Stage,
ed. Richard Foulkes, 1986, p. 244.

•

Fluellen has a problem, Booth's Theatre, New York, 1875.

The leek-eating has to be done near the footlights, and pretense is impossible. A property leek with a tube in which a piece of apple was inserted was the usual method employed, and Mr. Bishop, who had a great aversion to onions in any form, ate the apple without discomfort, but one night the property leek was lost or misplaced; a real leek was substituted, and poor Bishop had to eat the nauseating vegetable at which his stomach revolted in full view of the audience.

Frederick Warde, *Fifty Years of Make-Believe*,
New York, 1920. p. 102.

Elena Modjeska

Actress, 1844–1909

It was in the summer of 1880 that I played with [Elena] Modjeska for the first time, under romantic and novel conditions. She and her husband, Count Bozenta Chlapowski, and I, with my sister, were staying at the remote fishing village of Cadegwith, in Cornwall. The rector of St. Ruan hard-by urged us to give a performance in aid of his church, and it was decided, as there was no room or hall within miles big enough for such an audience as Modjeska would draw from the country-side, that the performance should be given in the rectory garden and at night. With the aid of the coastguards, a platform was made, near a running stream, with great trees as a background, and a big lawn gently rising from the brook became the auditorium. We gave some scenes from *Romeo and Juliet.* The lighting came from screened oil-lamps and the lucky help of a full moon. No stage balcony was ever so beautiful. It was full of mystery and charm, and Modjeska seemed to be inspired by the beauty and novelty of the surroundings. The big audience sat enraptured.

Sir Johnston Forbes-Robertson,
A Player in Three Reigns, 1925, p. 99.

Barry Sullivan
Actor, 1821–1891

. . . why did Barry Sullivan, after his early successes in America, Australia, and in London, shake London's dust from his feet, and play only in the English provinces, Ireland, and Scotland? It was because his forerunners all finally exhausted their London vogue there in a few years and were driven back to the road. The well known London manager Hollingshead declared that Shakespeare spelt ruin; and nobody contradicted him. Speeches longer than 20 words were considered impossible. Meanwhile Sullivan in the provinces was playing Hamlet, Richard, Macbeth, and Lytton's Richelieu over and over again to crowded houses, making £300 a week. He played Hamlet, his favourite part, more than 3000 times, and died a very rich man. Irving held out in London for thirty years and was driven back to the road penniless.

George Bernard Shaw, letter to Alan S. Downer, 21 January 1948; *Bernard Shaw: Collected Letters 1926–1950*, 1988, p. 812.

Barry [Sullivan] was giving this impersonation one night at Portsmouth to an audience largely composed of the breeziest of British sailors, who had been 'revelling' before arriving. After listening to the tragedy of *Hamlet* with commendably little interruption, suddenly, when Barry started 'To be or not to be' one of the Jack tars in the gallery stopped him, and shouted, 'Hi, Barry, give us a hornpipe!'

Barry scowled, as only he could scowl, at the irreverent interrupter, and started to continue his soliloquy, when several other Jack tars took up the cry, and said, 'Yes . . . give us a hornpipe, Barry! . . .' Then added a deep-voiced mariner, 'Mind as it's the sailor's one!'

This demand being repeated rather peremptorily Barry felt it his duty to step down to the footlights and to reprove these dance demanders! Having done so, he returned to the throne chair and resumed the great soliloquy on Life and Death, when a Herculean tar from a corner of the gallery shouted, ''Ere, Barry! . . . are you going to give me and my friends that hornpipe or am I to come down and make yer?'

Barry, by this time inwardly convulsed with laughter at this extraordinary joke, retorted: 'Gentlemen, as you insist upon my performing a Sailor's Hornpipe in the midst of this sublime tragedy, I will e'en do so.'

And Barry did it! And he did it well, for, like most of the tragedians of his time . . . he had gone through the theatrical mill so much and had played Black-Eyed Susan's William so often, that to dance a hornpipe at a moment's notice was the most natural thing in the world.

Having thus performed this famous dance to the tune of 'Jack Robinson', Barry Sullivan resumed his tragic and touching impersonation of Hamlet without further interruption!

H. Chance Newton,
Cues and Curtains Calls, 1927, p. 223

Samuel Phelps

Actor, 1804–1878

It was during an engagement of a few mornings at the Imperial Theatre that the catastrophe occurred.

He had always a superstitious dread of the word 'farewell'.

At the time of Salvini's desertion, I urged Phelps to play his farewell engagement, but he refused, alleging that he had dreamt that he should die on the stage if he attempted a farewell speech.

During the performance of *Henry VIII*, while acting Wolsey, while actually uttering the ominous words

> Farewell! a long farewell to all my greatness!

he broke down, in utter collapse, and the curtain as it slowly descended shut him out from the public gaze for ever.

John Coleman,
Players and Playwrights I Have Known, 1890, I, 205.

•

An 1882 production of *Macbeth* . . . brought two mishaps for William Rignold as Macbeth, one comic, one tragic. Contemporary newspaper cuttings tell the story:

> When, after an unconceivable pause, he began the famous soliloquy, 'Is that a dagger I see before me?', a cat sedately strolled upon the stage to form his opinion on the subject, and the presence of the harmless, necessary animal as it investigated the stage and the auditorium and peered down to see if there were any mice in the orchestra, was not found to assist the solemnity of the act.

A few evenings later, Dame Fortune frowned again.

> Just before the closing of *Macbeth* at Drury-Lane Theatre on Wednesday night, Mr William Rignold was accidentally stabbed in the chest by Mr J. H. Barnes. While the actors were fencing in the last act, Mr Barnes, instead of thrusting his sword in the side of his opponent, accidentally thrust it into his chest. A doctor was immediately called, and it was found the wound was rather serious.

Brian Dobbs,
Drury Lane: Three Centuries of the Theatre Royal 1663–1971, 1972, pp. 159–60.

Dame Madge Kendal

Actress, 1849–1935

and

W. H. Kendal

Actor, 1843–1917

Shaw reports on *As You Like It* at the St James's Theatre, starring Madge Kendal as Rosalind and W. H. Kendal as Orlando.

I have just been to *As You Like It.* If you want matter for a Palmeresque paragraph you may describe poor Rosalind's bad cold. Exposure in the Forest of Arden and an immutable resolution not to blow her nose before the audience did their deadly work; and at her exit in the third act she made a mistressly stroke of business out of them. She fainted, slipping from the neck of Linda Dietz with a beautiful stage fall in the patent collapsible manner. Orlando, with unconcealed scepticism as to the cause of the tragedy, and brutally marital blindness to its timeliness and attractiveness, bundled her off promptly. Well might she ask in the next act whether she had not counterfeited excellently. It was the only good piece of acting I saw.

George Bernard Shaw, letter to William Archer, 16 March 1885; *Collected Letters 1874–1897*, ed. Dan H. Laurence, 1965, p. 126.

Sir Frank Benson

Actor-manager, 1858–1939

Frank Benson acts Paris to Irving's Romeo, 1882.

I really could fence rather well, and I knew that I was a better swordsman than anyone else in the cast. I thought that when the fencing scene with Romeo came I should get a chance of showing off. That old weakness, love of showing off and playing to the gallery! I had also studied death spasms at St. George's Hospital. My one chance of distinguishing myself did not materialize. My efforts at fencing were too correct to be convenient for the old theatrical use of the rapier, and Irving seemed to fear that Paris's correct opposition might endanger Romeo's eyesight. Therefore with one hand he seized my foil, hit me over the knuckles with his own, prodded me in the stomach with his knee, again dashed his blade against mine, said, 'Die, my boy, die; down, down,' elbowed and kneed me into the mouth of the tomb, and stood in front of the dying Paris, brandishing a torch, amidst shouts of applause for Romeo, and little, if any, regret for Paris.

The dying thoughts of Paris were that so far he had failed to reform the elocution and the sword-play of the Lyceum.

Sir Frank Benson, *My Memoirs*, 1930, pp. 173–4.

Frank Benson put on *The Tempest* as part of his season at the Lyceum Theatre, London, 1900.

FRB played Caliban, one of his favourite performances. He spent many hours watching monkeys and baboons in the zoo, in order to get the movements and postures in keeping with his 'make-up'.

His old nurse saw him one night, dressed in this curious costume, and exclaimed, 'Oh, Mr Frank, you are the image of your sister in that dress.' . . .

FRB delighted in swarming up a tree on the stage and hanging from the branches head downwards, while he gibbered at Trinculo, and I must say this was a most effective piece of business.

Constance Benson,
Mainly Players: Bensonian Memories, 1926, p. 179

Stratford enjoyed *The Winter's Tale* more than the Bensonians did . . . This revival [1903] seems to be remembered principally because Benson, who had a long wait as Leontes, left the theatre during the revels in Bohemia, slipped a coat and trousers over his costume, and went for a row on the Avon. Miscalculating, he arrived back just as his cue was spoken on the stage. There was no time to think. Still in grey flannel trousers he rushed on, realised his mistake – helped by the frenzied whispering of the stage manager – rushed off, and returned with some dignity, as the King of Sicilia, to enter on the appropriate phrase, 'I am ashamed.'

T.C. Kemp and J. C. Trewin,
The Stratford Festival: A History of the Shakespeare Memorial Theatre, 1953, p. 63.

Sport in the country makes me think, too, of Sir Frank Benson. I suppose no actor who ever lived has been such an all-round athlete as this old 'Varsity Blue. It is said of him, that, if he were debating which of two actors to engage for a certain part, the slightly inferior artist, if he was a fine cricketer, would most certainly have obtained the coveted honour of employment under the Bensonian banner.

I have heard, though I cannot vouch for the story, that Sir Frank's contracts with his artists were always worded: 'To play the Ghost in *Hamlet* and keep wicket,' or 'To play Laertes and field cover-point'; and it was said that no Polonius need apply unless he happened to be a first-class wicket-keeper.

Sir Seymour Hicks,
Me and My Missus, 1939, p. 114.

F. R. Benson was knighted in 1916, Shakespeare's Tercentenary, after a special performance of *Julius Caesar*.

When F.R.B. came to Drury Lane on May 2, he must have known that a dozen Bensonians would be acting in the named cast of *Julius Caesar* (Ainley as Mark Antony), and thirty in the ensuing Shakespeare Pageant. But we can be doubtful whether the arithmetic would have engaged him, even if his mind had not been fraught. At eleven o'clock on the morning of the performance, which would begin at one-thirty, he and Constance sat in a hotel lounge at Victoria. A letter was brought in. As we know, strange things could happen to F.R.B.'s correspondence: this letter, sent earlier to his old office in Henrietta Street, had just caught up with him after a delayed progress from place to place. Opening it, he found that he had been offered the honour of knighthood.

That was not entirely a shock. Rumours had been drifting at Stratford-upon-Avon, and several telegrams of congratulation had arrived: all premature and, so F. R. B. believed, misinformed. It was never easy for him to imagine honour to himself; he had shrugged off the idea and got on with rehearsal. Here now was proof. Writing an explanation and grateful acceptance, he sent an uplifted Joe Richmond to deliver this at Buckingham Palace. The plenipotentiary came back defeated. His Majesty was at luncheon; the letter must wait. Troubled, for silence might have been misinterpreted as discourtesy, the Bensons drove to Drury Lane where F.R.B. called on the manager, Arthur Collins, also Master of the day's Shakespeare Pageant. 'Leave it to me', Collins said, and Benson, still disturbed, went to dress. Presently King George V and Queen Mary arrived.

. . . As soon as their Majesties were in the Royal Box, Collins went to Sir Charles Cust, the aide-de-camp, told him the story, and asked if the King could knight Benson that afternoon. His Majesty, Sir Charles demurred, was not in uniform, and had no sword. Collins begged him to speak to the King. A sword would be provided, and not a property weapon. Calling apart R. H. Lindo, the secretary of Drury Lane, Collins said: 'Benson is to be knighted. Run round to Simmon's and borrow a sword.' Lindo rushed off into Covent Garden. A sword? To lend to the King? It sounded preposterous; but a telephone call to Drury Lane settled doubt, and presently the imperative Lindo returned with his sword, a modern type with a khaki hilt. Sir Charles, approving of it, warned Collins that to knight Benson in the theatre would be impossible. It seemed to Collins the most reasonable place: an actor's accolade for gallantry on his own field of battle. He asked Sir Charles to explain to the King, and news was hurried to Benson. While Constance waited with other actresses in one of the big dressing-rooms, F.R.B., his Caesar having thrice refused a kingly crown, beckoned her out to him. 'The King', he told her, 'has consented. I am to be knighted in the Royal Box.' At the end, summoned from his dressing-room on the first floor of the O.P. side of the theatre, Benson crossed the stage and by corridor and stair reached first the ante-chamber of the Royal Room, and then the Room itself behind the Royal Box. There he knelt before the King, still with the bloodstained robes, the painted white face, the sunken eyes, the blue lips and lines of pain, and the half-bald wig of the dead Caesar. That day, lacking enough greasepaint, he had smeared the hollows of his face with dust and dirt. 'I naturally felt nervous,' he said, recalling it later, 'but I glanced up as I knelt in an old nightshirt, with dust all over my face, and I saw a twinkle in the eyes of the King and the Queen.' A few seconds later he rose as Sir Frank: the creation (said *The Times*) 'of a knight by title of one who has been all his life a knight by nature, vowed to the service of his Gloriana who is England.'

J. C. Trewin,
Benson and the Bensonians, 1960, pp. 215–16.

F.R. Benson had a season at the Lyceum Theatre. It seemed to me rather ridiculous. I saw him as Caliban in *The Tempest* . . . Benson's idea of Caliban was to come on stage with a fish between his teeth.

Edward Gordon Craig, *Craig on Theatre*,
ed. J. Michael Walton, 1983. p. 165.

When I was playing the Queen in *Hamlet*, surrounded by Bensonians who knew every line of every play in Shakespeare (not to mention every pitfall), they told me that there was a slip which the Queen was liable to make. I dared them to tell me of it but eventually extracted from them the promise that it should be revealed to me only on the day of the last performance. I had forgotten about it and found myself on the last night surrounded by these serious students of Shakespeare incapable of holding back the secret any longer. Feeling confident that nothing would shake my knowledge of the words, I said, 'Come along, what is it?' and they said, 'Take care when you say your first line that you don't misplace the words, "Good Hamlet, cast thy nighted colour off," and say instead, "Good Hamlet, cast thy coloured nightie off"!'

Irene Vanbrugh, *To Tell My Story*, 1948, p. 100.

•

The Duke of Saxe-Meiningen, whose company displayed highly disciplined ensemble playing, was a prototype of the modern director.

. . . But Chronegk, the Duke's producer, had a passion for literal truth which sometimes resulted in effects which seemed a little strange. For instance, when the Meiningen company performed *Julius Caesar* at Drury Lane during a later visit to London in 1891, some of the critics were puzzled as to why the clouds which during the Forum scene gradually veiled the view of the Capitol drifted across the stage only a foot or two from the ground. Chronegk, replying to a critic who assumed that the clouds had got a little out of control, explained that 'it must be borne in mind that the Forum Romano, or Campo Vuecino as it is now called, is situated at a considerable elevation and that, therefore, the clouds which lowered and frowned upon Rome on the night preceding the death of Caesar must have been at a very low altitude to obscure the Capitol and the higher buildings of the city from view.'

Norman Marshall,
The Producer and the Play, 1975, p. 141.

Ada Rehan

Actress, 1860–1916

Ada Rehan appeared in the opening production of Daly's London Theatre, 1893.

Ada Rehan, as you see her in the picture at Stratford-upon-Avon, made a magnificent entrance. One heard a noise off like an engine's whistle. It grew nearer and nearer, the curtains burst asunder, and there was Katherine. A Shrew before one even saw her . . .

Sir Barry Jackson, quoted in J. C. Trewin, *The Birmingham Repertory Theatre 1913–1963*, 1963, p. xiii.

Constance Benson

Actress, 1860-1946

Constance Benson plays Doll Tearsheet for Benson's company.

This part many people tried to dissuade me from playing, but I had watched a living 'Doll Tearsheet' in a drunken brawl one night in Manchester, and was most anxious to turn my copy to account. The Press were good enough to say many complimentary things of my performance, but several clergymen preached against me in Stratford-upon-Avon and elsewhere in the strongest terms, though one of them owned to having come more than once to see the performance.

Nowadays no one would be shocked, but in 1894 it was thought highly immoral to 'make vice attractive'. Some years later this play was most unwisely chosen for a matinée in Malvern. Our audience consisted mainly of schools, and in the middle of the 'Tavern-scene' the schoolgirls were ushered out in a body by their outraged mistresses.

I received several indignant letters the next day, one of which concluded with the following words: 'I would never watch you again as "Juliet", knowing to what depths you can sink'!

Constance Benson,
Mainly Players: Bensonian Memories, 1926,
pp. 124–5.

Louis Calvert

Actor, 1859–1923

At Manchester we were playing *Julius Caesar*, Louis Calvert, a most earnest actor, was Brutus. O. B. Clarence and I were playing Varro and Claudius [*sic*] in the tent scene. Before the curtain went up Calvert turned to us and said 'Don't cod to-night, boys, I'm inspired.' That finished him. When Brutus cried out after the exit of Caesar's ghost, 'Varro, Claudius, fellow thou awake,' Clarence and I rose and faced Calvert and in one eye, the blind one to the audience, we each had a monocle. But he asked for it.

Oscar Asche, *Oscar Asche His Life*, n.d., p. 95.

Julia Neilson

Actress, 1868–1957

She triumphed as Rosalind in Sir George Alexander's production of *As You Like It* at the St James's Theatre in 1896–7.

In later years Julia often told her friends how she had enjoyed playing it. Abhorring a wig, she wore her own hair clubbed into a 'bob'. They gave her Arne's setting of 'The Cuckoo Song' out of *Love's Labour's Lost* and she sang it delightfully. Once, when she spoke her lines in the Epilogue: 'If I were a woman I would kiss as many of you as had beards that pleased me, complexions that liked me and breaths that I defied not,' an eager voice came down from the gods: 'Me first, please, Miss!'

W. Macqueen-Pope,
St. James's Theatre of Distinction, 1958, p. 148.

•

. . . I have many times in my stage experience, before and behind the scenes, seen and been concerned with several condensed versions of *Hamlet* in which we used a real dog star to work the *dénouement*.

These 'Dog Hamlets' (as they were called) were mostly played by clowns and pantomimists of note at their benefit time. Then Mr. Merriman would don Hamlet's inky cloak, and would go through the real text of the tragedy in a condensed form and would play it for 'all it was worth' plus its famous performing dog! This faithful sleuth-hound was first brought in while the Ghost was giving his son a description of this 'murder most foul'.

The talented animal was next introduced in the play scene to keep its 'eye' on the guilty Claudius, especially where that murderous monarch is caught out by Hamlet's 'Mousetrap' matinée.

The lynx-eyed dog finally was brought into the corner to watch during the fencing bout of Hamlet and Laertes, and when that murderous trick was disclosed, the dying Dane called his dog forward and that canine star at once leapt at the throat of the gory sovereign and pinned him to the earth until he perished miserably!

H. Chance Newton,
Crime and the Drama, 1927, pp. 85–6.

Sir Barry Jackson

Director, 1879–1961

I recall . . . during amateur days, a *Twelfth Night* with John Drinkwater as Malvolio, with rapidly diminishing audience, and a rapidly approaching thunderstorm. Only two old ladies, huddled together under an umbrella, remained while I hissed to the protesting Malvolio: 'You must go on, or we shall have to repay their money.'

J. C. Trewin,
The Birmingham Repertory Theatre 1913–1963,
1963, p. 14.

William Poel

Actor, director and author, 1852–1934

[William Poel] cast each part according to a preconception regarding the voice of the character, like a conductor orchestrating a chorus. For his *Twelfth Night* in 1897 he attempted to make Viola a mezzo, Olivia a contralto, Orsino a tenor, Sebastian an alto, Malvolio a baritone, Toby a bass, and poor Andrew a falsetto. He seemed to care little for the actual playing so long as the vocal music was right.

Dennis Kennedy,
Granville Barker and the Dream of Theatre, 1985,
p. 150.

He [Bridges-Adams] found Poel wrapped in a grey muffler, nibbling at a biscuit and sipping a glass of milk. In front of him a lady, shimmering with sequins and no longer in her first youth, was in an attitude of visible distress. Poel's voice was raised in querulous criticism: 'I am disappointed,' he said, 'very disappointed indeed. Of all Shakespeare's heroes Valentine is one of the most romantic, one of the most virile. I have chosen you out of all London for this part, but so far you have shown me no virility whatsoever.'

Robert Speaight,
William Poel and the Elizabethan Revival, 1954,
p. 121.

It was not until 1932 that I had a chance of working with Poel in a Shakespeare play. He had become interested in *Coriolanus* and he invited me to play the leading part. If I had asked myself – or anyone else for that matter – whether I was suitable casting for Coriolanus, the answer would have been a resounding negative. But that was not the kind of question you put to yourself when Poel asked you to work with him. All Poel's productions were in the nature of laboratory experiments, and you were content, for the time being, with the status of a privileged guinea-pig . . . Of all Poel's productions, this production of *Coriolanus* was probably the most eccentric. At an early stage he opened his mind to me about the costumes. He thought the public was tired of togas, and I said that I was tired of them too. Seeing the play as inspired by the fall of Essex – for Poel most plays were inspired by the fall of Essex – he might well have decided to put it into Elizabethan dress, and the idea would have had much to recommend it. But no, he had decided to play it in the costume of the French *directoire*. This was a period of political and military ferment, and *Coriolanus* was this kind of play. The notion appealed to me; I am much happier in breeches than in togas or tights. But then an unfortunate thing happened. Poel went to see the exhibition of Italian painting at Burlington House and came away obsessed by the picture of a young man in a leopard skin. It was thus, he insisted, that I must make my first entrance; and from that moment on any pretense at sartorial consistency went by the board. I pleaded that God had not designed me for leopard skins, but no – Poel wrote that he wanted me to be 'an emblem more than a personage', and the leopard skin would have this further advantage that my sword would be of necessity unsheathed. Since it was not in the character of Coriolanus to imitate other people, he must therefore be dressed quite differently, and it was all that I could do to prevent Poel bringing me back from the wars in an eighteenth-century uniform and powdered wig. What he did was to bring me back in the full-dress uniform of a Colonel of the Hussars!

Robert Speaight, 'A Memory of William Poel',
Drama Survey, 1964, p. 502.

Mrs Patrick Campbell

Actress, 1865–1940

She played Lady Macbeth to James Hackett's Macbeth at the Aldwych, 1898.

Sir David Webster, the director of Covent Garden Opera House, tells me he has always treasured her remark about Hackett's Macbeth: 'When he opens his mouth he spits at me, and whenever I speak he clears his throat.' James Agate told me, often and often, that Mrs. Campbell used to complain loudly at the rehearsals about having to sit on a green log in a puce dress while Macbeth did all the talking. 'Well, well,' said the director, anxious to mollify and keep the peace, 'I'll ask Mr. Hackett to *pat* you once or twice.' Whereupon Lady Macbeth is said to have replied in tones of infinite melancholy: 'I *hate* being patted!'

. . . As late as 1937 Mrs. Campbell sent to Shaw from New York a recollection of how the stately-prim and puritanical Dame Madge Kendal came to see the *Macbeth*: 'She came on the stage, taking no notice of me, and when I thought she had flattered Hackett enough I said to her: "And how did you like my *street-walking* scene, Mrs. Kendal" – you remember Hackett wouldn't let me play in an antechamber but insisted that I walk on the ramparts – her mouth twitched – she had a sense of humour – she asked me to luncheon next day – I knew better than to go.'

Alan Dent, *Mrs. Patrick Campbell*, 1961, p. 165.

Robert Mantell

Actor, 1854–1928

A burst of applause greeted Mantell as Richard, as he slithered out in front of a plain curtain. 'Now is the winter of our discontent,' Mantell began, but before he finished his line, down from the flies came a flurry of paper snowflakes left over from Miss Bingham's snowstorm to settle on the cloak of the crook-backed tyrant. Mantell controlled himself, waited out the titters and choked guffaws of the audience, and continued. After another half-a-dozen lines he suddenly lurched forward, narrowly keeping his balance, and the audience stirred again. On the shallow front Mantell was forced to play close to the curtain, and a diabolic stagehand concealed behind it had tried to pitch Mantell into the laps of the front-row patrons. Mantell again recovered and somehow got through the scene.

The tumult of shouted orders, dropped props, and stagehands 'tripping' noisily over stage braces continued unabated until Mantell's next soliloquy. Nearly mad with rage, Mantell had still managed to keep himself under control on stage. But now, he saw the form of a man backstage print itself against the curtain, preparing, as he surmised, to send the actor headlong into the audience. Mantell thought quickly and, making the business fit the lines of his text, thrust his dagger, a real one, through the curtain. There was a cry, which went unnoticed by the audience because of the accompanying din, and then silence. Mantell discovered after the scene that he had wounded the stagehand in the leg and threatened similar treatment to the rest of the crew, if another sound from backstage was heard for the duration of the performance. Nobody took up the challenge.

Attilio Favorini, '"Richard's Himself Again!": Robert Mantell's Shakespearean Debut in New York City',
Educational Theatre Journal, 1972, p. 408.

•

I have often heard the players prompted in the text by kind friends in front at the 'Wells,' but perhaps the most extraordinary case was during one of Pennington's performances as the Prince of Denmark. Some of my relations were often called upon (as I was myself in later years) to 'go on' at a moment's notice for several parts a night, in this and other Shakespearean plays, with the acting editions of which we were all familiar.

On one of such nights a cousin of mine, who had been playing Rosencrantz and other parts with which he was pretty well acquainted, suddenly had to deputize as Osric, a part with which he was not too familiar. By way of 'ponging' it the poor chap slipped a French's copy of *Hamlet*, opened at Osric's part, in the hat which that contemptible courtier has to flourish so much round about him.

Thus, by glancing more or less closely into his chapeau, this Osric deputy was able to get along pretty well. Suddenly, however, he came to a stop at a word he couldn't catch. Whereupon a very kind-hearted galleryite, leaning over the prompt side and noticing the book in Osric's hat, cried out, 'Spell it, old pal! We'll tell you what it is!'

H. Chance Newton,
Cues and Curtain Calls, 1927, pp. 221–2.

Lewis Waller
Actor, 1860–1915

Every bit of Waller acted . . . He would arrive upon the scene full tilt. Indeed, he began his entrance well off stage. He would lean against the farthest wall and just before his actual cue came, give himself a push off with his heel and travel towards the door, archway, or whatever it was through which he had to go. He never just stepped on the stage – he came upon the scene like a breath of fresh air . . . And, being an experienced actor, he mostly entered from up-stage centre, and not from the side, thereby making an impact.

W. Macqueen-Pope,
Ghosts and Greasepaint, 1951, p. 102.

William Mollison told me that as a small boy he was in his father's dressing-room one night during the original run of Waller's *Henry V*. It was the night when Queen Victoria's death was announced, and Waller entered Mollison's dressing-room with a face of grief, suddenly bursting into tears and crying 'She's dead, Bill, she's dead!' Mollison tried to comfort him and begged him not to take it too much to heart. But Waller was inconsolable. 'It's the receipts, Bill', he sobbed: 'the receipts are bound to drop.' They did.

Hesketh Pearson,
The Last Actor-Managers, 1974, p. 44.

•

Arthur Machen played the conjurer Bolingbroke in Benson's *The Second Part of King Henry VI*. Later he was asked to help Matheson Lang play 'the old magician'.

The actual spirit I had to raise [in I. iv] was Lily Brayton, who was then a very beautiful, etherial-looking young girl . . . Benson, knowing Machen's interest in magic, black and white, asked him to give me a form of incantation that would be suitable. This Machen taught me; a long Latin invocation which took me a terrible time to learn.

When we came to the first night, Machen wished me luck.

'But be careful of that invocation,' he said, 'it's a real one, you know. Goodness knows what you may raise when you speak it.'

Matheson Lang,
Mr. Wu Looks Back: Thoughts and Memories . . .
1941, pp. 34–5.

The version [of *Richard III*] I played was, of course, Shakespeare's not Cibber's. It is amazing how long the bombastic fustian of Cibber held the stage, and how hard his version was to dislodge from it. Edmund Kean, who made his great success in Cibber's version, revolted at last and tried to force Shakespeare, pure and unadulterated, upon the public; but they would have none of it, and he had to return to Cibber. The oft-quoted line 'Off with his head! so much for Buckingham!' which according to tradition never failed to bring down the house was Cibber's.† I think Irving was the first to win over the public for Shakespeare's unspoiled, original version.

†The applause which followed this absurd line was naturally very precious to the actor who was playing 'Richard'. Harry Loveday, whose father had played with Kean, told me a good story. One night a small part player, from sheer nervousness, rushed on to the stage and shouted 'My Lord, the Duke of Buckingham is taken and we've cut off his head.' Kean, absolutely nonplussed, could only murmur: 'Oh! . . . then there's nothing more to be said.'

Sir John Martin-Harvey,
The Autobiography of Sir John Martin-Harvey,
1933, p. 381.

Upon one occasion I received practical instruction in the importance of conviction in acting. We were playing *Hamlet*, and an argument arose because the previous night the leading lady had tangled up her words and said something rather silly, and the audience had laughed. Listening to the discussion was our oldest actor; he once had played Hamlet, was now playing the King, and would doubtless finish up as the Second Gravedigger. 'You can say anything, my boy,' he interrupted me, 'provided you say it with proper conviction. Now I'll bet you a pint of beer that I will say something quite absurd in the next act, and no one will laugh.'

Rashly, I took the bet. Nothing happened until just before the duel between Hamlet and Laertes, when the King concludes his instructions to the duellists with the words: 'And you, the others, bear a wary eye.' Fixing me with a glassy stare – I was playing Horatio – the old actor said: 'And you, the others, wear a beery eye.' This was received in stony silence. When I returned to the dressing-room our King was waiting for me. All he said was: 'Laddie, my pint.'

Basil Dean, *Seven Ages*, 1970, p. 42.

Sir Herbert Beerbohm Tree

Actor-manager, 1853–1917

When Tree played 'Hamlet' in Manchester, there was an amusing episode one night. Hamlet lay dead on the stage, and Tree had arranged an unseen chorus of angels, to sing his soul to rest. This was generally very effectively done under the direction of Raymond Roze in the wings, but on this particular occasion Roze had gone up to London on business connected with the forthcoming production of *Trilby*. So the 'Angels' started their chorus without a conductor. Unfortunately, they all sang in different keys, and the effect was so horrible that the 'dead' Hamlet was heard to groan furiously.

On went the chorus, going from bad to worse, and the dead Hamlet's groans provided a running accompaniment. At last the late Prince of Denmark could stand it no longer.

'Oh those —— angels!' cried the corpse furiously.

The curtain fell at last, and the instant it fell the 'Angels' bolted, and locked themselves in their dressing-rooms, till they were assured that Hamlet had left the theatre. And I know that this story is true, for my wife was one of the '—— angels'!

W. H. Leverton,
Through the Box-Office Window, 1932, pp. 57–8.

Of Tree's spectacular Shakespearean productions, *Richard II* gave me a fine chance – in my opinion, one of the best I have ever had, the gratifying result being that I appeared to satisfy all concerned. An unexpected difficulty, with a decidedly humorous flavour, cropped up in connection with this piece. One of the scenes was laid on the Welsh coast, my conception of it showing a bay, with hills in the distance, much of the local colour being afforded by a recent visit of mine to Barmouth. In the foreground I painted a mass of golden Plantagenet broom, which brought me, if I may say so, a good deal of commendation.

To heighten the effect a quantity of real broom was ordered to be strewn on the stage, or, failing it, a suitable substitute. As the poet has it, 'someone blundered,' and blundered sadly, the stage at one of the final rehearsals being strewn not with broom, but *gorse*!

The result was that when at the line, '*Let's talk of graves, of worms and epitaphs*;' the lightly-clad king threw himself in his grief to the ground – well, you might search your Shakespeare through and through and not find any of the lines uttered on this occasion!

Joseph Harker,
Studio and Stage, 1924, pp. 136–7.

An actor in his company reported that he had been to a matinée of *King Lear* at the Haymarket theatre. 'Good house?' asked Tree. 'Pretty good, but there seemed to be a lot of paper.' On which Tree, in Falstaff's voice, quoted *The Merry Wives of Windsor*: 'I see. "The leer of invitation"!'

Hesketh Pearson,
Beerbohm Tree: His Life and Laughter, 1956, p. 185.

Sir Herbert Tree asked me to play Hotspur with him at His Majesty's Theatre in his production of *Henry IV*, Part 1 . . . At the first rehearsal, he said to me:

'Of course you are going to stutter in the part.'

'Stutter?' I asked. 'Why?'

'Oh, don't you know,' said Tree, 'a German actor, playing in a production recently in Berlin, got the idea from a reference in the text to Hotspur's stammering and stumbling over his words.'

This idea seemed a very effective one, and I jumped at it. Hotspur in his violent outbursts of rage might easily have stuttered and stammered. So we set to work. For over three weeks Tree taught me how to stutter, and almost every morning he had a different theory. One day he would say:

'You mustn't sound the consonants. For instance, in the word Bolingbroke (which occurred frequently in the part), no stutterer would sound the "b", just O-O-Olingbroke.'

So I set to work on that idea. A morning or two later Tree would pull me up again:

'No, no, no, you must stutter on the "b", he would say. 'B-B-B-Bolingbroke.'

So we went on, and I had finally arrived, with considerable difficulty, at a mastery of this very complicated and difficult business. The day before the production we had a final dress rehearsal, a *répétition général*, with some hundreds of friends present. The next morning at seven o'clock I was wakened from a deep sleep by my telephone ringing. I crawled grumpily to the phone. It was Tree at the other end.

'Oh, Lang, for God's sake cut out that stutter.'

'What?' I shouted down the telephone. 'For God's sake, why?'

'Some of my friends thought it was nervousness and that you were drying up. So you'll have to cut it out.'

At this I went off the deep end.

'Look here, Sir Herbert, for weeks you have been teaching me how to do this damn' stutter, and if you expect me to cut it all out on the day of production and play the part straight without it, I just simply can't do it.'

'You're very difficult,' said Tree, 'and very argumentative.'

'I'm nothing of the kind,' I replied, 'but if you really think so, you had better put the understudy on to play the part tonight because I am sure *I* couldn't do it with all the stuttering left out.'

So finally he had to give way and the stutter was kept in, and the next morning, to my delight, I found that almost every critic on the London Press had approved of it and hailed it as a very effective innovation.

Matheson Lang,
Mr. Wu Looks Back: Thoughts and Memories . . .,
1941, pp. 120–2.

I had a serious argument with Sir Herbert [Beerbohm Tree] at the dress rehearsal, almost amounting to a quarrel. It was absurd as I look back at it, and it has made me laugh many times since, but when it happened I took it very seriously. He loved historical facts and had discovered that Cleopatra had five children. This appealed to his whimsical, fantastic mind. What was my horror to find myself in the procession, looking most lovely, followed by this brood! What could an actress do? The splendid, passionate Queen was ridiculous with a large family. The domestic point of view of Cleopatra seemed utterly incongruous. I simply couldn't bear it. I implored him to take them away, but he insisted on all five at the dress rehearsal. How could one be romantic under those circumstances? It was no use making that glorious entrance to be followed by those children, getting smaller and smaller, like steps, until the last one was quite tiny.

I was broken-hearted, and wept so bitterly, stamping my foot and making a ridiculous scene and saying I would not play, that at last he gave way to pacify me, and we compromised on three.

I prepared for my entrance on the first night with three following behind.

I tried to look as if they did not belong to me, and prayed in my soul that the audience would think they were attendants. I treated them with great scorn. I mounted my throne and looked around, and the two smallest, gorgeously robed in silver, looking like miniatures of me, were coming hand in hand, bewilderment on their little faces.

He had given them a star entrance and made it worse than ever. If ever there was murder in my heart it was at that moment; I could have willingly strangled my entire family.

Those children were always a bone of contention between us, and spoilt my enjoyment of the part, but it was Sir Herbert's everlasting joke. He teased me throughout the run of the play.

I would mount the steps with the greatest dignity to find a doll sitting on my throne with 'Ptolemy Junior' pinned on its chest. He would put them in my room, or on my dressing table, or there would be dolls, dressed up, in some quiet corner of the stage, leaning sideways, looking ridiculous. And one night, in one of the very serious scenes, he slipped a little naked doll into my hand.

Constance Collier, *Harlequinade*, 1929, pp. 186–7.

The most versatile actor on the stage of my time was Lyn Harding, who during Tree's Festivals appeared in such widely diverse parts as Aguecheek in *Twelfth Night*, the Ghost in *Hamlet*, Cassius in *Julius Caesar*, Prospero in *The Tempest*, Ford in *The Merry Wives*, and Bolingbroke in

Richard II, playing each in a masterly manner. Once he acted Tree and everyone else off the stage. He was Enobarbus in *Antony and Cleopatra*, and at the fiftieth performance the whole house cheered him. Tree continued to appear before the curtain taking all the calls meant for Harding, until at length the entire audience united in a single yell of 'HARDING', when the lights went up and the National Anthem was played. This cannot have been pleasant for Tree; but he maintained his policy of getting the best actors for the best parts and letting them speak as many of their lines as the spectacular mounting permitted.

Hesketh Pearson,
The Last Actor-Managers, 1974, pp. 17–18.

In one respect Tree certainly overdid his staging. That was in certain plays having any forest – or alfresco – scenes. He loved to engage real animals! This was especially the case with *The Merry Wives of Windsor* and *A Midsummer Night's Dream*. In the woodland scenes in these two plays real deer, real pigeons, real hares and rabbits – not to mention squirrels – were 'specially engaged' to add realism to the general effects. Mostly, these zoological stars behaved in such a manner as to call for 'the sack' without the usual fortnight's notice!

Still, Tree could never be cured of this fondness for engaging real game, ditto vermin, etc. In spite of his rather trying experiences with animals in *The Merry Wives of Windsor* and in his first revival of *A Midsummer Night's Dream*, on his second revival of the latter play – when he gave up the part of Bottom to Arthur Bourchier – he proudly introduced a large number of real rabbits into the scene representing 'A Wood Near Athens.'

Now, it so fell out that one of these professional rabbits kept annoying Bottom Bourchier so much that he had to drive it from the stage – much to the delight of the audience! At the end of the act, Bourchier, on taking his call, brought that refractory rabbit on under his arm. Suddenly – again to the delight of the audience – that rabbit turned furiously and bit Bourchier!

Recently Bourchier, in referring to Sir Herbert and his and my happy times with that lovable humorist, said to me, 'But do you know, I never could understand why that d——d rabbit tried to gnaw me!' 'Surely it was obvious,' I replied. 'It was from professional jealousy!'

H. Chance Newton,
Cues and Curtain Calls, 1927, pp. 149–50.

As a producer he had no equal. His sense of beauty, his sense of the stage, and his ability to make crowds of 'supers' come to life and behave like real actors has never been surpassed. There was nothing about the stage which he did not understand. Once they were rehearsing a thunderstorm. A real one blew up outside and after a crash of real thunder Tree said it would not do. They told him it was real thunder. 'Ah,' said Tree, 'that may satisfy the people outside but we must do better at Her Majesty's.'

W. Macqueen-Pope,
The Curtain Rises, 1961, p. 292.

At rehearsals of *Macbeth* he made some famous cracks. He had real Guardsmen for the armies in the battle scene. These men entered into the spirit of the fight with gusto and laid about them so heartily that their swords chopped pieces off the scenery and smacked against the backcloth. 'Soldiers, soldiers,' shouted Tree. 'Listen to me. Never hit a backcloth when it's down.' And later, when an over-zealous soldier had inflicted a slight flesh wound on his stage opponent, he declared: 'I make a ruling. Any one soldier found killing any other soldier will be fined.'

W. Macqueen-Pope,
Carriages at Eleven: The Story of the Edwardian Theatre, 1947, p. 41.

. . . No doubt it is an exaggeration to say that the only unforgettable passages in his Shakespearean acting are those of which Tree and not Shakespeare was the author. His Wolsey, which was a 'straight' performance of high merit and dignity, could be cited to the contrary. But take, for examples, his Richard II and his Malvolio. One of the most moving points in his Richard was made with the assistance of a dog who does not appear among Shakespeare's *dramatis personae*. When the dog – Richard's pet dog – turned to Bolingbroke and licked his hand, Richard's heart broke; and he left the stage with a sob. Next to this came his treatment of the entry of Bolingbroke and the deposed Richard into London. Shakespeare makes the Duke of York describe it. Nothing could be easier, with a well-trained actor at hand. And nothing could be more difficult and inconvenient than to bring horses on the stage and represent it in action. But that is just what Tree did. One still remembers that great white horse, and the look of hunted terror with which Richard turned his head as the crowd hooted him. It passed in a moment; and it flatly contradicted Shakespeare's description of the saint-like patience of Richard; but the effect was intense: no one but Chaliapin has since done so much by a single look and an appearance for an instant on horseback. Again, one remembers how Richard walked out of Westminster Hall after his abdication.

Turn now to the scenes in which Shakespeare has given the author a profusion of rhetoric to declaim. Take the famous 'For God's sake let us sit upon the ground, and tell sad stories of the death of kings.' My sole recollection of that scene is that when I was sitting in the stalls listening to it, a paper was passed to me. I opened it and read: 'If you will rise and move a resolution, I will second it – Murray Carson.' The late Murray Carson was, above all things, an elocutionist; and the scene was going for nothing. Tree was giving Shakespeare, at immense trouble and expense, and with extraordinary executive cunning, a great deal that Shakespeare had not asked for, and denying him something much simpler that he did ask for, and set great store by.

As Malvolio, Tree was inspired to provide himself with four smaller Malvolios, who aped the great chamberlain in dress, in manners, in deportment. He had a magnificent flight of stairs on the stage; and when he was descending it majestically, he slipped and fell with a crash sitting. Mere clowning, you will say; but no: the fall was not the point. Tree, without betraying the smallest discomfiture, raised his eyeglass and surveyed the landscape as if he had sat down on purpose. This, like the four satellite Malvolios, was not only funny but subtle. But when he came to speak those lines with which any old Shakespearean hand can draw a laugh by a simple trick of the voice, Tree made nothing of them, not knowing a game which he had never studied.

George Bernard Shaw,
'From the Point of View of a Playwright',
Herbert Beerbohm Tree: Some Memories of him and of his Art, collected by Max Beerbohm,
n.d., pp. 242–3.

Beerbohm Tree was knighted in 1909, by which time his friend Herbert Asquith had become Prime Minister.

Maud [Lady Tree] liked to give the impression that Herbert's knighthood was a great surprise. It was probably only a surprise to Herbert who remarked that he hoped he would not be expected to become genteel. Maud said he could be a very parfait but not a genteel knight. A friend who was writing to congratulate both Maud and Herbert, before Herbert had been 'dubbed', asked Max [Beerbohm] whether she should address Maud as Lady Tree. The reply was that it seemed to be correct as she was already Lady Tree 'in the sight of God'.

. . . By a careful *coup de théâtre* Tree was acting Malvolio in *Twelfth Night* when his honour was publicly announced. As he reached the lines, 'Some have greatness thrust upon them' the house 'rose' to him.

. . . When the accolade was about to be bestowed by King Edward, Herbert and Arthur Pinero were waiting in an ante-room for the touch of the sword. Pinero said to Herbert: 'Do you think we could have it done under gas?'

Madeleine Bingham,
'The Great Lover': The Life and Art of Herbert Beerbohm Tree, 1978, pp. 183–4.

•

The playing of Shakespeare used to be far more traditional, and relatively fixed, than it is today.

Even in this century there is a story of an old actor who, invited to perform Kent in *King Lear* at a provincial theatre, wrote back accepting and saying 'Usual moves, I suppose?'

Stanley Wells, 'The Academic and the Theatre',
The Triple Bond, ed. Joseph G. Price, 1975, p. 9.

. . . you never knew what made me play Juliet with such tenderness and passion. I will tell you the secret now: It was Romeo. It was H. B. Irving. It was hopeless and unrequited love. For was not Irving's heart already given to another? With what a heaving bosom and with what shining eyes I went on to the stage for my performance of Juliet! The ballroom scene: Romeo will fall in love with me. His eyes like burning coal will light on mine. He wears his father's beautiful Romeo costume, his limbs, carved out of turquoise. Romeo sees me, comes towards me. I await with longing heart and downcast eyes. He will speak to me. He will say: 'If I profane with my unworthiest hand/This holy shrine . . .' He doesn't, but whispers fiercely: 'What the devil do I say?' Good-bye Romance! Farewell Romeo! I pull myself together. 'Feed' Romeo with his cue. Henceforth I can be nothing more than a mother to him.

Lillah McCarthy,
Myself and My Friends, 1933, p. 41

Konstantin Stanislavski

Actor, director, teacher, 1863–1938

Stanislavski worked first with a semi-professional company, *The Society of Art and Literature*. In 1896, he directed *Othello*.

The production plan was detailed and elaborate, with the text marked up in different colours in a code to which the key has been lost. Stanislavski was well aware that everything depended on the quality of the production and not on the modest talents of the cast. Busy as he was with other productions – notably a much-improved revival of *A Law Unto Themselves* – with his business and his family, he needed quick results. Those who could not deliver the goods had to be dragooned into doing what he wanted. He had not yet acquired the ability to draw out performances from his actors. When all else failed he followed the old dictum: when an actor is weak, create a diversion. His Iago, although a professional, was just such a case. During one of his more important soliloquies he found himself practically unlit while Stanislavski brought on a doorkeeper with a lantern to distract the audience's attention from a tedious moment.

Jean Benedetti, *Stanislavski, a Biography*, 1988, p. 52.

Nonetheless, the Society served its purpose. Stanislavski amply justified his stand over staying in Moscow and using the Society as a springboard. The final season provided an attractive foretaste of what the Art Theatre would be able to offer. Two major new productions were presented, *Twelfth Night* and *The Sunken Bell*.

Twelfth Night opened on December 17, 1897. The production was well received. It seemed to the critic of the *Russkoe Slovo* that the cast played like a full orchestra under a great conductor. There was not one false note, not one harsh sound. It was neither too fast nor too slow. Stanislavski's Malvolio on the other hand, ran contrary to the traditional view, and was less well received. Like many twentieth-century interpreters he saw the dark side of the character. The same critic found that:

'. . . he made the audience pay attention to him rather longer than they should, endowing him with strong feelings. The pleasure Malvolio took in the letters he received and then his indignation and rage were too strong, too tempestuous for this insignificant pedant and so, instead of drawing laughter, Malvolio drew pity.' (*Russkoe Slovo*, January 6, 1898).

Jean Benedetti, *Stanislavski, a Biography*, 1988, p. 52.

Lilian Baylis

Manager, 1874–1937

Lilian Baylis devoted her life to making the Old Vic Theatre, London, a popular home for drama. Edward Gordon Craig had his doubts about the audience's taste for Shakespeare.

Romeo and Juliet was always a nerve-wracker for the audience – and for me. They didn't like the love-making – neither did I. They would whoop and cat-call at anything, because it got on their nerves. And when Romeo, after getting the poison from the apothecary, tells the sky that he is going back and will lie with Juliet tonight – meaning, naturally, that he will kill himself with her, they whooped as though we had somehow slipped through the fine net of the censor of plays.

Once, I remember, on this tour, the spectators even had an attack of nerves in *Hamlet* – on seeing Hamlet holding a skull in his hands as he said, 'Alas, poor Yorick!' I don't think the publishers will allow me to put into print exactly what somebody yelled out; but evidently audiences are shaken by these very solemn things and it somehow doesn't agree with them. Why Miss Baylis should have decided to *make* it agree with them ('They *shall* come to heel, they *shall* like – what they don't like') I have never been able to understand.

Edward Gordon Craig,
Index to the Story of My Days, 1957

Miss Baylis was very exercised in her mind about a proposed production of *Henry V*. Ben Greet had told her it was just the play to draw all the soldiers in London . . . She said the only thing she knew about the play was The Prayer. She then asked me if I could kneel. Thinking she was about to ask me to play Henry, I told her that at present I couldn't kneel or walk, but that I hoped to get better soon . . . She then knelt down by the roll-top desk, with one hand resting upon the base of the telephone. The prayer which followed was exactly like a business talk over the 'phone. The 'Dear God' she addressed seemed to be on the other end of the line. She told Him who she was and what she was praying for, and hoped that in the presence of the soldier home from the front, He would listen. She asked Him if it was right to do *Henry V*. It was a long cast and would need more actors, and that meant spending more money. The last sentence of the prayer was that God should send her some good actors – and as an after-thought she added the word 'cheap.'

Sybil and Russell Thorndike,
Lilian Baylis, 1938, pp. 125–6.

Harley Granville-Barker

Director, actor and author, 1877–1946

Granville-Barker directs *The Winter's Tale*, 1913.

He knew exactly what he wanted from each actor. I was astounded, and I think the rest of the cast was, too, at my being chosen for Perdita. I had thought of her as a little Botticelli nymph (some kind of vague association with the *Primavera* I suppose), the daughter of a king. But Barker saw her as a country girl, brought up by a shepherd, and my puppy fat was if anything an asset . . . at the first rehearsal, when I was so shocked, the prim little prude I was, at the dress Albert Rutherston had designed for me that I refused to put it on. 'It's split right up one side, away up above the knee,' I cried to the wardrobe mistress. 'It will go right up to my waist when I dance. *Please* stitch down to just *below* the knee.' 'Oh! Miss,' said the horrified wardrobe mistress, 'you can't go muckin' about with a dress Mr Rutherston designed special, I won't put a stitch in it.' I waited till she was out of the room and cobbled it up, or should I say down, myself. I expect Rutherston howled in protest, but as he told me long afterwards when we had become friends, Barker, who used to be furious when people 'cheapened' a design by wearing a wrong hair style or whatever, just laughed: 'Don't worry, we'll snip it up again gently – she's got an odd quality of innocence which is quite different from ignorance. I don't want that spoilt.' . . . Playing Perdita, I ceased to hanker so much after a Botticelli figure with long slender legs, and resigned myself more to my puppy fat.

Cathleen Nesbitt,
A Little Love and Good Company, 1975, pp. 63–4.

Barker rehearsed his company almost to weariness, urging them until his sensitive ear was satisfied, to speak swiftly but to remember the musical structure of the verse. All must be rapid, continuous, intimate, vital. He sent round twelfth-hour typed cards for the players to hang by their dressing-room mirrors. Arthur Whitby's, for Autolycus, read: 'BE SWIFT. BE ALERT. BE DEXTEROUS. PITCH THE SONGS HIGH. BE SWIFT. BE ALERT.'

J.C. Trewin,
Shakespeare on the English Stage 1900–1964,
1964, p. 53.

Like all exceptional men, he has his fads. One of them is that he expects his artists to suggest things in their parts as well as he can suggest other – more terrible – things at rehearsal. To give an example. He was rehearsing me for the part of Valentine in a revival of *Twelfth Night* that didn't mature. Valentine has a speech in which he gives a message from Olivia to Orsino. I, very naturally, rendered the speech exactly as given me by (presumably) Maria. The actual words are: 'But from her handmaid do return this answer.' But that wasn't good enough for Barker. Oh, no! He explained to me at great length, and (I regret to say it) quite unconvincingly, that part of the speech was Maria's own, that Malvolio had probably touched it up in places, and that Sir Toby Belch had unquestionably put a phrase in here and there. He didn't tell me how all this was to be suggested, short of imitating the voice and manner of the various authors, so I failed to give it Barker-justice. He ruffled his hair, executed a *pas de seul*, and eventually (not, I hope, on account of me) substituted another play.

Hesketh Pearson,
Modern Men and Mummers, 1922, pp. 168–9.

But when Barker tackled Shakespeare and Shaw he broke down. Those two dramatists demand colour, sound, movement, the flourish of rhetoric, everything in fact that does not in the least resemble the humdrum life of the suburbs; and though Barker brought off some exquisite moments in the quieter and more lyrical passages of Shakespeare, the plays as a whole evaded him. As Shaw said, he hated acting, and managed to get something else. I recall an amusing episode when his instructions were swept aside without a word of explanation or excuse by Tree, who was acting Antony in the Forum scene from *Julius Caesar* at the Coronation Gala Performance in 1911. Barker, having by then achieved considerable prestige in the theatrical world, was asked to produce the scene. The crowd consisted of some three hundred actors, well-known and unknown, who packed the arcade behind His Majesty's Theatre when they used it as a dressing-room for the performance. Barker had gone to great trouble to prepare a pamphlet of some twenty-four pages in which the movements of every member of the mob were carefully noted at each stage of the proceedings: e.g. 'X 186 groans heavily and moves up stage, where he joins a doleful group consisting of Ys 48–54 and Zs 201–10', or something of that sort. It was a remarkable effort and must have cost Barker many weary hours of thought; but he had overlooked the simple fact that it would have taken about two months' hard rehearsing to get the effect at which he aimed. His early frantic efforts, with the aid of a powerful bell, to control the crowd of 'stars', 'semi-stars' and 'walking gentlemen', were about as successful as would be an attempt to secure order in a monkey-house into which a few elephants, tigers, peacocks and parrots had strayed. After two or three desperate and chaotic rehearsals, Tree came on the scene. Barker's pamphlets were promptly scrapped, and Tree's simple method was adopted of letting the rabble do what they liked when given free rein, while attending in dead silence to Antony whenever he was orating.

Hesketh Pearson, *The Last Actor-Managers*, 1974, pp. 75–6.

Granville-Barker directs *King Lear* at the Old Vic, 1940.

Barker knew when a great shout of laughter was valuable – when Goneril asked Edmund for a kiss he was allowed to bestow it with such passion that she was left swooning, and when he had gone from her sight and she turned to face the approach of her fussy timorous elderly husband, her sigh of 'Oh what a difference of man to man!' made the audience laugh so much that they almost felt a wave of tolerance towards her. And, when Albany in rage having discovered her treacheries towards the King, shouted that only her woman's shape could shield her from his hands: 'Apt enough to dislocate and tear thy flesh and bones' her impudent answer: 'Marry! Your manhood? mew' was another laugh when as Barker suggested, she started a little 'mew' like a kitten and ended half-giggling and a full-throated 'miaou!'; puncturing poor Albany's rage as a child punctures a balloon with a pin.

Cathleen Nesbitt,
A Little Love and Good Company, 1975, p. 194.

Harley Granville-Barker as director.

He still had a great feeling that people mustn't ever think that any part was too small. I do remember when Lear comes on at the very end carrying Cordelia, and the Captain of the Guard comes on with him. And Lear says: 'I killed the slave that was hanging her with my own hands.' Or lines to that effect. And the Captain says, "'Tis true, my lord, he did' – and he just sort of *said* it. Barker came up to him and withered him with a glance and said: 'My dear young man, you're under the impression that you've got one line to speak and this is not a very good part. I assure you it is of the utmost importance. To begin with, I noticed that when you came on with Lear you just came on and stood. You should hardly be able to stand. Do you realise that you have seen a miracle? Think of what people do when they see a miracle. They don't know whether to believe it, they don't know whether they're on their hands or their feet, their hearts begin to beat. You have seen a miracle. This very old man, you know what he's been through, and he kills a man with his own hands, and then picks up a hefty young woman and comes onto the stage carrying her, and so when you say ''Tis true,' you must realise that you are accepting that you've seen a miracle and that the world is a very strange place.' He gave him a little lecture about this. There is no line in Shakespeare that is extraneous.

Cathleen Nesbitt,
'Cathleen Nesbitt talks to Michael Elliott about Harley Granville-Barker',
The Listener, 13 January 1972.

Curiously enough, just as my memory of the beginning of the War is linked with Granville-Barker, so is that of the end of it. He and his wife came to dinner with me the night peace was declared. I had just played *Hamlet* in London for the last time, and I knew that they had been to see the play. But Granville-Barker refused to talk about the theatre at dinner. Instead, his wife chattered about her dog which was in quarantine, some Spanish poetry which she had translated and all sorts of other things. However, after dinner, when we went upstairs, Granville-Barker took me into a corner. Having thanked him for the help he had given me in the Elsinore *Hamlet*, I told him that there were certain things I did not like in the current production. 'In my first scene I have to sit on stage looking at the audience, whereas you made me come late to the council table and doodle on my papers and fidget – it was so much more original and effective.' Granville-Barker replied: 'Oh I'm afraid we didn't see the first act, because we were late; we'd had a late lunch.' This upset me, rather naturally. He began to look very sleepy and soon after he and his wife left in a taxi. About a week later he wrote me a charming letter in which he said some very nice things about my Hamlet; but he would never have been late for the first act of *Hamlet* in the old days.

Sir John Gielgud,
An Actor and his Time, 1981, p. 126.

•

One of them [the Bensonians], 'Walter Plinge', would never be out of work. He does not figure on the Lyceum list; but it was at the Lyceum, or very near to it, that he began. H. O. Nicholson wrote to a friend in August 1939: 'Yes, I believe I am responsible for Walter Plinge's adopting the stage as his profession. W. P. was actually born in 1900 during the Bensons' season at the Lyceum. He appears in the cast lists a few years later.' Strangely, he did not reach a Birthday programme at Stratford-upon-Avon until 1912, when he gave his usual steady performance of Agrippa in *Antony and Cleopatra*; but he had been soldiering in the provinces for many seasons before this. ('M. Plinge', clearly a relative, was the Porter in the *Henry VIII* of 1902.) The original Plinge, who kept a public house close to the Lyceum stage door, was a tolerant and helpful landlord much liked by the company. His name would appear on a fantastic number of programmes; he is said at one point to have played three parts simultaneously in three different London theatres, and he could be trusted to carry with resource, and at the same time, any kind of spear required at Inverness or Bath.

J. C. Trewin,
Benson and the Bensonians, 1960, pp. 120–1.

Russell Thorndike

Actor, 1885–1972

Russell [Thorndike], who had been invalided from the Army, joined the Vic company in 1916, and there is no more famous story from Waterloo Road than that of the *Lear* night during an air-raid. Striding downstage, with Sybil's white-faced Fool at his heels, Russell's Lear cried 'Crack Nature's moulds, all *Germans* spill at once!' as the Zeppelin rode high above London and bombs crashed down upon Waterloo Station.

J. C. Trewin, *Sybil Thorndike*, 1955, pp. 40–3.

•

Sir Cedric Hardwicke answers an interview question, 'What is the most moving moment you remember in the theatre?'

Seeing Ellen Terry when she was close to eighty years old playing in the trial scene of *The Merchant of Venice*. As she approached Portia's 'quality of mercy' speech, her face went suddenly bleak and lost. She struggled vainly for a moment, then moved down to the footlights. 'I am a very silly old lady,' she said, 'and I cannot remember what I have to say.' Almost to a man, the audience shouted the lines and cheered as she smiled her thanks and returned to her place. She played the rest of the scene to an enthralled audience.

Sir Cedric Hardwicke,
A Victorian in Orbit, 1961, pp. 307–8.

Nigel Playfair's tradition-breaking production of *As You Like It* at Stratford-upon-Avon (April 1919) was notable for Claude Lovat Fraser's 'Futurist' designs.

When the curtain rose the audience were puzzled perhaps, but they listened with respect and attention. But it was outside the theatre that the storm raged, and it attained a ferocity I should hardly have thought possible. When I came into my hotel I was certainly treated as a 'national criminal': people turned their backs – got up and walked out of a room which I came into. The rest of the cast fared little better: they were cut and cold-shouldered almost everywhere. Where Lovat Fraser himself was walking in the street a woman came up to him and shook her fist in his face. 'Young man,' she said impressively, 'how dare you meddle with Our Shakespeare!'

Nigel Playfair, *The Story of the Lyric Theatre, Hammersmith*, 1925, p. 55.

And I must not forget in making this brief record that one of the great causes of offence at Stratford was that I did not allow a very ancient stuffed stag to be carried on in the Forest Scene, a stag that was kept in the Museum for the purpose, and was expected to make its appearance. One must not of course flout the traditions of a particular theatre. Who was it who told me that he was appearing as quite an ordinary man of his own age at an East End theatre, and replied in answer to a question of his dresser that he did not propose to wear a wig? The dresser was horrified. 'I shouldn't do that if I were you, Sir! They look for a wig here.†

†Sir John Martin-Harvey reports the Elder Clarkson: 'In my young days, wigs were WIGS, *now* they want them to look like the 'air of the 'ead.' *The Autobiography of Sir John Martin-Harvey*, 1933, p. 45. Wire-beards used to be employed.

Nigel Playfair, *Hammersmith Hoy*, 1930, p. 207.

But the late Robert Atkins is said to have used his understudy in an original way. Atkins was Enobarbus in *Antony and Cleopatra* and his understudy was his page. (Shakespeare allows for no such attendant.) One night, in a famous passage, Robert Atkins dried: it was the description of the first meeting of Antony and Cleopatra. He turned to his page/understudy and said 'Philomel, tell thou the tale.'

Clive Swift, *The Job of Acting*, 1984, p. 61.

In 1924 the calls for the return of the platform stage were growing stronger.

A real platform stage would confer many benefits on Shakespearean actors. Among the chief of these would be the Freedom of the Clown. The Elizabethan clown is hand-in-glove with the audience. Again and again he addresses the groundlings. At present this intimacy is severely hampered by the proscenium. The little apron at the Old Vic is a very poor apology for a platform . . . but it is better than nothing, and it was upon this apron that Mr. Hay Petrie, when playing Launce in *The Two Gentlemen of Verona* a few months ago, actually had the temerity to wink at a gentleman who gave a belated laugh in a private box. This liberty on the part of Mr. Petrie – a liberty he could never have taken from the back of the stage – created a small sensation among the critics . . . It is, indeed, the most important thing that has happened at the Old Vic during the past year.

Herbert Farjeon, *The Shakespearean Scene: Dramatic Criticisms*, 1949, p. 183.

John Barrymore

Actor, 1882–1942

He plays Hamlet in London, 1925.

One thing that enchanted Jack with the *Hamlet* play was the physical leeway it permitted the actor. 'You can play it standing, sitting, lying down, or, if you insist, kneeling. You can have a hangover. You can be cold-sober. You can be hungry, overfed, or have just fought with your wife. It makes no difference as regards your stance or your mood. There are, within the precincts of this great role, a thousand Hamlets, any one of which will keep in step with your whim of the evening. Why, one night in London, after I had been overserved with Scotch at the home of – never mind her name – I got halfway through my 'To Be' soliloquy when it became expedient to heave-ho, and quickly. I sidled off to the nearest folds of the stage draperies and played storm-at-sea. I then resumed the soliloquy. After the performance one of the fine gentlemen who had sponsored me for membership in the Garrick Club confided: 'I say, Barrymore, that was the most daring and perhaps the most effective innovation ever offered. I refer to your deliberate pausing in the midst of the soliloquy to retire, almost, from the scene. May I congratulate you upon such imaginative business? You seemed quite distraught. But it was effective!' To which I replied: "Yes, I felt slightly overcome myself."''

From *Good Night, Sweet Prince (The Life and Times of John Barrymore)* by Gene Fowler, p. 210.

•

Barry Jackson's celebrated 'modern-dress' production of *Hamlet* at the Kingsway Theatre, 1925, encountered some informed criticism of the clothes worn.

The Men's Wear Organiser had something to say about the clothes. The sartorial expert was very upset about the Prince, who was 'in the air' in regard to his rig-out. 'His evening kit was a sheer disgrace. The soft shirt and soft double collar, worn with a suit which does not appear to be even the correct evening-dress material, are abundant evidence that his mind is just a little deranged.' But his plus-fours were admired, and the writer liked 'the double-breasted suits worn by Laertes, Horatio, and the *jeunesse dorée* of the Danish Court.' *The Tailor and Cutter* also had a word to say on the subject; suggesting that Hamlet's fondness for a dinner jacket and soft collar when everyone else was in full evening-dress made him look like 'a peevish provincial boy, unaware of the etiquette of dress.' It is amusing to notice that *The Outfitter*, faced with a production in which 'there were few sartorial errors of real importance,' criticised the 'glaring sartorial mistakes' made by members of the audience, especially a few of the daily paper critics. 'In a first night of this nature,' the writer complained, 'it is hardly the thing to wear an ill-fitting "dicky", as one of the gentlemen did.' Fortunately, Sir Frank Benson was 'elegantly dressed,' and Bransby Williams wore a 'dinner jacket-suit of excellent cut,' and there were other actors present who gave tone to a house that was let down by the critics!

G. W. Bishop,
Barry Jackson and the London Theatre, 1933, p. 54.

Macbeth at the Old Vic, 1926.

This production was however doomed in more ways than one; Ainley, having survived a ten-hour dress rehearsal, was taken ill early in the run and replaced by Hubert Carter who, though a long-time reliable stalwart of the Casson company, allowed the role to go to his head and, nightly in the duel scene, all but killed Basil Gill as Macduff until Lewis had stage-hands posted out of sight among the scenery to hiss at Carter during the duel that Macbeth was intended by the author to lose it.

Sheridan Morley, *Sybil Thorndike: A Life in the Theatre*, 1977, p. 89.

Theodore Komisarjevsky

Director and designer, 1882–1954

Komisarjevsky's production of *King Lear* for the Oxford University Dramatic Society (1926) was the pilot for his landmark *King Lear* at Stratford-upon-Avon (1936–7).

Keen Shakespeareans will readily recall that the Duke of Cornwall's servant, although not a very large part, has one highly important and spectacular scene of which, I flatter myself, I made the most. The honest fellow, appalled by his master's treatment of the unfortunate Gloucester, bids him stay his hand, is promptly set upon by the incensed Duke and, after a prolonged sword-fight, slain. Thanks to the Mappin Terraces with which Komisarjevsky had filled the entire stage – a device which in those days, at least in England, was looked on as revolutionary – the sword-fight, for which we had received special training from the University sabre champion, became one of the highlights of the production and each night I confidently awaited the horrified intake of breath with which my dying fall from the topmost ledge was regularly greeted. That I survived a week of this, relatively intact, was due to luck, careful timing and the maintenance of strict precautions in the matter of body-armour; others were not so fortunate, or so careful, and Peter Fleming, ever impetuous, on one occasion, when he had scorned to put on his helmet, received a nasty crack on the head from my four-foot blade (steel, not papier-mâché) and on another, having forgotten his mail gauntlet, received a wound which lent dramatic emphasis to his exit-line, 'I bleed apace!' Nor was he the only victim, for one night as I swung Excalibur over my left shoulder a loud groan signalled that I had dealt an effective back-hander to one of those old men whom Shakespeare so frequently leaves hanging about the stage, invariably in one of the pools of darkness without a superfluity of which no continental producer can possibly make do. The very next evening my trusty weapon finally failed, snapping off smartly at the hilt, flying across the stage, tearing through a flat and, after narrowly missing Miss Martita Hunt who was playing Goneril, buried itself in the prompt-side wall.

Osbert Lancaster,
With An Eye To The Future, 1986, pp. 66–7.

Sir Ralph Richardson

Actor, 1902–1983

He [James Agate] was unfortunately also deeply prejudiced by the time Richardson began to be known (and that he could be spiteful, obnoxious, and opinionated, also goes almost without saying). He couldn't, for a start, waive his view that an actor's personality was wholly dependent on his physical limitations. This may be arguable, but in Agate's case the view was carried to extremes: so-and-so could never be Hamlet – he didn't look the part. It was a romantic and homosexual view. Agate's first talk of Richardson after meeting him socially, and lunching with him at the Savage Club in 1932, is significant: 'A year or two ago Richardson had the habit of acting all his parts with his buttocks. I cured him of this, and his Henry V had no backside at all, though it reappeared, and rightly, in his next comic part.'

Richardson showed, by lunching with Agate at the Savoy Grill, or his other haunt, the Ivy, that he was at least conversant with the diplomatic processes by which one achieved notices. George Howe, who had scrupulously avoided Agate at the Savoy in the belief that actors and critics shouldn't mix, recalled being told: 'Ah, you're the young man who refuses to meet me. Didn't you know I never give an actor a good notice unless I've been introduced to him first!' But Agate also took advantage of knowing actors, and could be very indiscreet and embarrassing. Gielgud recalled his coming to his dressing room in 1929, during the first interval of *Macbeth*, and saying: 'I have never seen the murder scene better done, so I have come to congratulate you now. At the end of the performance I shall probably have changed my mind, for you can't possibly play the rest of it.'

Gary O'Connor,
Ralph Richardson: An Actor's Life, 1982, pp. 66–7.

Max Reinhardt

Director, 1873–1943

Reinhardt's last production in England was *A Midsummer Night's Dream* for the Oxford University Dramatic Society, in the summer of 1933. It is said that Reinhardt, on surveying the site, said: 'Very nice. But –' indicating the Headington rooftops in the distance – 'that village over there must be removed!'

Large, alarming wheels began to turn. Cables arrived. The Herr Professor Doktor would like 'eighty extras and a lake'. (He was at the time producing the play in Florence, where there were far greater resources than we could possibly offer.) And, equally disconcerting, he would like to produce the play on a hill. Hills are not two-a-penny in Oxford. For a start, this knocked out the grounds of all the colleges, many of which were quietly but keenly competing for the honour. Eventually we obtained the use of Headington Hill, just beyond Magdalen Bridge – and a wonderful site it proved, with a foreground area of meadow, a row of sparsely placed but thick trees behind it, through which was seen a further meadow, and a wood to one side.

. . . As for Max Reinhardt's spontaneity, to which I have already referred, we had abundant examples. When we were rehearsing on Headington Hill, University rules compelled us to be in our Colleges by midnight. At ten to twelve, on a signal from the stage manager, we used to break and run to our cars, leaving the great man shouting after us on the hill-top. To our great delight, this situation was used at the end of the first craftsmen scene: the craftsmen all ran off, leaving Quince yelling after them: 'Meet me in the wood', etc., purple with rage. And again, when, as Bottom, I was calling for my companions, Reinhardt discovered that, if I shouted in a certain direction, there was an echo from across the valley, and at once a double-take was added by my pulling the string attached to one of the ears of the donkey's head.

Most wonderful of all, though, was his direction of the 'Methought I was, methought I had' speech. Usually this seems to go for very little. With Reinhardt, it began with a nervous groping, to see if the long snout and the long ears were still there; then a quickening of gesture, a nervous laughter; a sudden cut to silence; a fifty-yard run to the pond; a look at the reflection in the water; a scream of relief; and a jubilant dance off through the trees towards Athens. I don't know what impression this gives in print, but I can assure you that every night it held the audience like a vice. And, to repeat what others have said, although every minutest gesture and moment of timing was controlled, I felt as if it welled up naturally from deep inside me. Reinhardt never imposed an interpretation; he evoked it.

As for the pictorial side, what was so impressive from behind the scenes was the simplicity with which the most powerful effects were achieved. At the play's opening, the lords and ladies just stepped out from behind the trees where they had been hidden. The whole landscape was suddenly, effortlessly alive. When the craftsmen first met, in the fading evening light, they started from the back of the further meadow, the jogging lights of their lanterns gradually converging, to the music that Mendelssohn wrote for them . . . Then there was the moment when Puck ran across the sward, and vanished, bringing a gasp from the audience every night. He had simply jumped into a pit, banked up so as to be invisible to the audience – from which his arm now came up, like a malevolent twig, to trip each craftsman as they came into the enchanted wood. When Oberon (Philip Arnhold) climbed into a tree to overhear the lovers, he disappeared, but the tree shimmered with a mysterious magic. And anyone who saw that production will remember the end of the Nocturne, when Nini Theilade, Reinhardt's exquisite little Danish dancer, was carried off into the night by Michael Martin Harvey, a slowly narrowing spotlight following the undulation of her hands to a pin-point of light in the darkness.

Felix Felton, 'Max Reinhardt in England,' *Theatre Research*, Vol. 5, No. 3 (1963), pp. 140–2.

In January 1905 the revolve was used to spectacular effect in Reinhardt's production of *A Midsummer Night's Dream*, a play to which he returned at least eleven times over the next thirty years. Reinhardt and his designer, Gustav Knina, divided the revolve into two contrasting areas: the 'real' world of Athens, represented by a marble arena, a courtyard before a palace, and a spacious hall for the concluding nuptials – and the wood, at once the natural habitat of the spirit world, a refuge for lovers, and a meeting-place for the mechanicals:

> Veritable trees, not painted but plastic ones, were placed on the stage, and the space below was covered, not with a painted ground-cloth, but with what seemed to be palpable grass, in which the feet sunk among the flowers; while here and there were seen bushes and little beeches growing between the trees, and in the midst of all a little lake mirrored between two hills.
>
> And now (constructed on the revolving stage) all this forest began slowly and gently to move and to turn, discovering new perspectives, always changing its aspect, presenting ever new images inexhaustible as Nature. And while the stage turned and changed, the elves and fairies ran through the forest, disappearing behind the trees, to emerge behind the little hillocks. These beings with their green veils and leafy crowns seemed, in their appearance, to form a part of the forest itself. Puck, who up to that time has been usually dressed in the costume of the fantastic ballet or opera, was covered only with grass and became at last the true elf, who rolled with laughter like a child in the green of the forest.

This was a revelation. Never had such unity between actor and stage decoration been seen. Never before, and in a manner so justified, had one seen the stage setting become an actor of such importance in the play. A new impetus had been given and a new intense life henceforth entered the modern theatre.

E. Braun, *The Director and the Stage*, 1982, p.99, including an extract from W.R. Fuerst and S.J. Hume, *Twentieth-Century Stage Decoration*, 1929 and 1967.

Charles Laughton

Actor, 1899–1962

He plays Macbeth at the Old Vic, 1933.

Charles and Miss Baylis ended up on speaking terms, but only just. At one time there seemed a chance that they would become quite friendly. Then came *Macbeth*. At the end of the first performance round to the dressing rooms comes Miss Baylis, aware of a need to administer cheerful but honest consolation to My Boys and Girls. Charles is in his room aware that the evening has not been a success, painfully aware that his own performance has fallen short of the promise of the dress rehearsal. If ever a human creature is vulnerable it is a leading man at the end of a long exhausting performance which he knows has been a disappointment.

Charles is at his dressing table, still made up as Macbeth. To him comes Miss Baylis in the full academic robes to which as an Honorary M.A. of Oxford she was entitled, and which she very sensibly put on for first nights: beaming benignly through her glasses upon the dejected actor, she gave what I knew was a laugh of embarrassment. Anyone who has been to a dressing room after a difficult first night will know that embarrassment. Charles declares it was a hyena's yell of triumph. She then caught him a smart crack across the shoulder blades.

'Never mind, dear,' she said, 'I'm sure you did your best. And I'm sure that one day you may be quite a good Macbeth.'

He never forgave her.

Tyrone Guthrie,
A Life in the Theatre, 1960, pp. 127–8.

[Charles Laughton] was quite open about his problems with the work, and was, Marius Goring admiringly observed, willing to try anything, not caring a fig whether it made him seem foolish. – At a certain point in rehearsals of *Macbeth*, for example, he came in in a state of great excitement: 'I've got it! I'm so sorry, I see it now: it's a *Scottish* play: Macbeth must be played Scots.' Guthrie: 'Interesting idea, give it a try.' After three days: Guthrie: 'It's no good Charles, worse than it was without, worth trying out.' So Charles gave it up. (The problem, Goring added, was that Charles couldn't do a Scots accent, anyway, it kept coming out Scarborough.)

Simon Callow,
Charles Laughton: A Difficult Actor, 1987, pp. 76–7.

Charles Laughton plays King Lear at Stratford-upon-Avon, 1959.

. . . his understanding of *Lear* led him to focus his performance on the second half of the play. In a letter to a young fan, he had described his anguish in the dressing-room; how he 'dreaded going through all the things Shakespeare had written: the terrible journey of Lear to his death.' That was the key-note for him: not the fall from a great height, not the turbulent rage, but the stumbling progress towards death. During the run of the play, he was troubled by nightmares associated with the play. He got his cousin, Jack Dewsbery, a psychiatrist, to come to see the performance: 'I went up to Stratford, and, for reasons which even now are unknown to me, I was struck by the very first speech he made in the play, in which Lear speaks of his coming death and of the need to dispose of his properties. I told Charles that was where I thought the trouble lay . . . I can only suppose that in some way his dreams had foretold the future, and that I had unwittingly put my finger on their meaning.'

. . . His attitude was almost detached; it was almost like a lecture. 'I know more about *Lear* than anyone living,' he'd mock-boasted, and his performance was a kind of instruction. There is one famous incident which is highly significant in this regard. At a certain performance half way through the first scene, he completely forgot his lines, and asked for a prompt. It came. No, no, he said, back to the beginning of the speech. Again came a line. No, no, he said again, further back. You see, ladies and gentlemen, he said, turning to the audience, this is *plot.* And then he resumed the performance, not at all fazed. The remarkable point, though, is that *neither was the audience.* He had created a relationship with them where they had placed themselves totally in his hands.

Simon Callow,
Charles Laughton: A Difficult Actor, 1987,
pp. 258, 264.

Fanny Rowe

Actress, 1913–1988

Following the obituary of Fanny Rowe in *The Times* of 3 August 1988, Richard David wrote (*The Times*, 10 August 1988):

At Cambridge her success as an undergraduate actress in a number of productions persuaded the Marlowe Society to abandon its rule that female parts should be played by men, and her outstanding Cleopatra, at only 20, ensured that in the future women would share in the society's performances.

This brought the following letter from Mrs Elizabeth Belsey (*The Times*, 17 August 1988):

Mr Richard David, in his comment on your obituary of Fanny Rowe, modestly does not mention that he was playing Antony to her Cleopatra. I wonder whether he remembers a notorious incident that took place during one of the performances.

Cleopatra had just died, and I, as Charmian, was about to die, too, when a young drunk rushed shouting from the wings on to the stage behind us. He was immediately seized and dragged out; but in the agitation of the moment I forgot my lines.

'It is well done,' hissed the corpse of Cleopatra, lying at my feet, and I recovered and continued.

When the curtain fell, we all sprang to life and ran off-stage to find out what had happened.

'It's all right', said a stage-hand soothingly. 'Don't worry, his trousers have *been* taken off.'

In the Cambridge of those days (1934) extreme disapproval of anybody's conduct was registered in this manner.

I have never known who the culprit was.

Sir John Gielgud

Actor, 1904–

Gielgud answers an interview question, 'Did you have any conscious model for Hamlet when you were studying the part for the first time?'

No, I didn't. I thought I had. I thought I would copy all the actors I'd ever seen, in turn, and by then I'd seen about a dozen or fifteen Hamlets. Of course, Irving was my god, although I'd never seen him; I'd just read about him being Ellen Terry's partner. But the whole idea of this magnetic strange man, whom I knew I could never be anything like, somehow appealed to me more than any other past actor that I'd ever read about. I didn't try to copy, I only took note of all the things he'd done and looked at the pictures of him, and so on. But when it came to the Vic, the play moved so fast and there was so much of it that I suddenly felt, 'Well, I've just got to be myself,' and I really played it absolutely straight, as far as I could. Of course, I was fortunate in that, except at Oxford, Hamlet had never been allowed to be given to a very young actor until I played it. It was the kind of prize that an actor, when he went into management at the age of forty or fifty, H.B. Irving or Baynton or whoever it was, allowed himself. I don't think anybody (except Master Betty) had ever played it under thirty-five, and it made people realize the tragedy of the beginning of the play in a way that an older man can never achieve. When I played it in 1944, at the age of forty, I was well aware that, with the help of various directors and actors with whom I'd worked over fifteen years, I knew more about the part, had better staying power, and perhaps more selectivity. But I didn't think I could contrive the opening of the play in the way that it had come to me when I was absolutely fresh, because I really felt it then; I was young and so I naturally put it over in the right way. But later I tried to imitate that, and I felt false. It always disturbed me that I was putting on my young voice and face and everything, for the beginning of the play.

John Gielgud, *Great Acting*, ed. Hal Burton, 1967, p. 140.

We had assembled for the first reading of *Measure for Measure* at Stratford. It must have been about 1950. I had never worked with John Gielgud before, nor had most of the actors. The occasion was nerve-wracking, not only because this time the reading was going to take place in the presence of a legend. Gielgud's reputation at the time inspired both love and awe and as a result each actor was thrilled to be there and dreading the moment when he would have to be seen and heard.

To break the ice I made a short speech, then asked the actor playing the Duke to begin. He opened his text, waited for a moment, then boldly declaimed the first line. 'Escalus!'

'My lord?' came the answer, and in those two words, hardly audible, one could hear the panic of an actor, wishing for the ground to open and playing safe with a token murmur.

'Peter!' From John came an impulsive, agonized cry of alarm. 'He's not really going to say it like that, is he?'

The words had flown out of John's mouth before he could stop them. But just as swiftly he sensed the dismay of his poor fellow actor and immediately was contrite and confused. 'Oh, I'm so sorry, dear boy, do forgive me. I know, it'll be splendid. Sorry everyone, let's go on.'

Despite his great gifts as a director, as an actor, he needs to be directed. When he develops a part, he has too many ideas: they pile in so fast, hour after hour, day after day, that in the end the variation on top of variation, the detail added to details all overload and clog his original impulses. When we worked together, I found that the most important time was just before the first performance, when I had to help him ruthlessly to scrap ninety per cent of his over-rich material and remind him of what he had himself discovered at the start. Deeply self-critical, he would always cut and discard without regret. When we did *Measure for Measure* he was inspired by the name of Angelo and spent long, secret hours with the wigmaker, preparing an angelic wig of shoulder-length blond locks. At the dress rehearsal no one was allowed to see him, until he came on to the stage, delighted at his new disguise. To his surprise, we all howled our disapproval. 'Ah!' he sighed, 'Goodbye, my youth!' There were no regrets and the next day he made a triumph, appearing for the first time with a bald head.

Peter Brook,
The Ages of Gielgud: An Actor at Eighty,
ed. Ronald Harwood, 1984, pp. 101, 103.

Then there was the tragic Hazel Terry, who once set light to herself in Gielgud's production of *The Winter's Tale* at the Phoenix. She was extinguished by the late John Whiting and Norman Bird, who were both playing small roles at the time. When Gielgud came down to the stage for his next entrance, he remarked: 'I hear cousin Hazel caught fire. The Terrys have always been combustible', before stepping out from the wings to resume playing Leontes.

Bryan Forbes,
That Despicable Race: A History of the British Acting Tradition, 1980, p. 270.

Geoffrey Kendal

Actor-manager, 1909–

Geoffrey Kendal describes the hazards of taking *Othello* on tour in India.

I remember telling Anwar, who was new to the company, to 'reduce the bulbs', as I wanted the footlights cut down for the final scenes of *Othello*. He obeyed all too readily. Iago was surprised to see, in mid-soliloquy, Anwar crawling round the side of the stage to the footlight, where he proceeded to remove bulb after bulb. Bowing to exigency, we played the murder scene solely by the light of the candle in Othello's hand. I am told it was strangely effective.

Anwar's appearance on-stage was not as unusual in India as it would have been in England. In the East the stage is not seen as being the preserve only of actors. With Chinese operas, for instance, when the heroine kneels down, one stage-hand will bring on a cushion for her and another will smooth out her train. There is no pretence that they are part of the play. An early example in our productions had been the canteen bearer with the bottle of lemonade, and there were a number of others. Once, in the middle of a tense scene between Othello and Iago, the dhobi, a pile of freshly laundered clothing on his head and an iron in his hand, came up to me on-stage and said, 'Dhobi finished now, sahib.'

Geoffrey Kendal with Clare Colvin,
The Shakespeare Wallah, 1986, p. 124

Peggy Ashcroft

Actress, 1907–1991

Katharine of Aragon, *Henry VIII*, Stratford-upon-Avon, 1969

Despite these initial uncertainties, Peggy had a very clear idea of the character she was playing. Indeed, not for the first time, her total immersion in a role made her almost proprietorial in her attitude towards it. 'Peggy herself,' Nunn recalls, 'had become obsessed with Katharine of Aragon to the point where she brought into rehearsals every day, a kind of defence of the character. She was on Katharine's side to the extent that she was against Shakespeare's. She would turn up with extra lines from the historical trial or from Katharine's letters and try and put them into the text. I had to argue that Shakespeare is not interested in that, so it doesn't matter if we are being historically inaccurate. Shakespeare is loading the dice and we have to help him. That is why Katharine is, to some extent, a tragic figure; she is much maligned in this version but the play goes on to other things. But, although we had minor disagreements, I don't think I ever argued Peggy out of her conviction that she was not playing Katharine but that she *was* Katharine.'

Michael Billington, *Peggy Ashcroft*, 1988, p. 224

•

The designer, Isamu Noguchi, was invited to work on *King Lear* for an extended tour finishing at the Shakespeare Memorial Theatre in 1955.

It was the costumes that caused the problem. Noguchi had never designed costumes before. He sent to Devine from New York paper maquettes painted and cut to scale. When the actors finally put them on at a dress parade at the Scala Theatre, the general reaction was one of horror. Lear himself appeared in a gown full of holes that made him look like a Gruyère cheese, his face was surrounded by a mane of white horsehair and on his head he wore a crown unkindly compared to an inverted hatstand. Honest Kent wore a leather jerkin surrounded by rubber rings that suggested a slightly depleted Michelin man.

Michael Billington, *Peggy Ashcroft*, 1988, p. 158.

Sir Michael Redgrave

Actor, 1908–1985

Vanessa Redgrave was born to Rachel Kempson while Michael Redgrave was playing Laertes at the Old Vic in 1937.

In the duel scene at the matinée, Olivier placed his foil against mine with infinite care and we pit-patted our way through the fight as in slow motion. Then, between the shows, came a telephone call from Blackheath, and the evening performance flew. When it came to the duel, though Laertes was far from steady on his feet, the fight was fast and brilliant. Larry at the curtain-call made a speech, as was the custom at the Vic on Saturdays, and announced, 'Ladies and gentlemen, tonight a great actress has been born. Laertes has a daughter.' The gallery roared their approval, and from the wings the student actors wheeled on a barrow of flowers with the message 'To Rachel and Michael – Love's Labour's Not Lost.' And after the show, at the Moulin d'Or, a favourite haunt for actors, Larry and Bobby Flemyng cleared a path for me through the tables, throwing flowers to the astonished diners and singing out, 'He's had a daughter.'

Michael Redgrave,
In My Mind's Eye, 1983, p. 108.

•

At the Old Vic they used to play the blinding of Gloucester as the first scene after the interval in *King Lear*, so that the craven-hearted could stay out until it was finished; and many of them did.

J. C. Trewin,
The Night has been Unruly, 1957, p. 262.

Orson Welles's production of *Julius Caesar* at the Mercury Theatre, New York, in 1937 operated under severe financial constraints. John Houseman cites a dialogue with Bill Baird, the puppeteer.

HOUSEMAN: Hey, Bill! That life mask for Caesar's corpse. It stinks! I'm sending it back!
BAIRD: What's wrong with it?
HOUSEMAN: It's beautiful. But it's two inches thick. How the hell can a boy lie for twenty minutes with that weight of plaster on his face?
BAIRD: Boy? I thought you were using a dummy.
HOUSEMAN: It has to be a boy! We can't afford a dummy!

John Houseman,
Run-Through, New York, 1980, p. 324.

Sir Tyrone Guthrie

Director, 1900–1971

A successful season ended with a nice loud bang and an invitation for the company to take our production of *Hamlet* to Elsinore to inaugurate an annual festival performance in the Castle of Kronborg.

. . . The opening was to be an important occasion – the Tourist Board had left no stone unturned. Royalty was to be present; a special train was chartered to convey the royal party and the diplomatic corps from Copenhagen. The press was there in force. And that night it rained as never before.

The performance was at eight; at seven-thirty the rain was coming down in bellropes. Miss Baylis, Larry Olivier and I held a council of war. It was out of all question to abandon the performance, indeed the special train had already steamed out of Copenhagen. To play in the open air was going to be nothing but an endurance test for all hands. We would give the performance in the ballroom of the hotel. There was no stage; but we would play in the middle of the hall with the audience seated all around as in a circus. The phrase hadn't yet been invented, but this would be theatre in the round.

Larry conducted a lightning rehearsal with the company, improvising exits and entrances, and rearranging business. George Chamberlain and I, assisted by the critics of *Dagbladet*, the *Daily Telegraph* and *Paris-Soir*, arranged eight hundred and seventy basket chairs in circles round the ballroom. Miss Baylis put on her academic robes and kept things going with royalty and ambassadors till we were ready.

The audience thought it a gallant effort and were with us from the start; actors always thrive on emergency and the company did marvels. But *Hamlet* is a very long play. After two hours of improvisation the actors became exhausted and a little flustered. The finale was a shambles, but not quite in the way the author intended. Still it had been quite a good evening; royalty looked pleased, ambassadors clapped white-gloved hands and the press next morning acclaimed a 'sporting gesture' and a *Hamlet* of more than ordinary vitality.

The performance would have worked better if we had been permitted to use all the entrances to the hotel ballroom. But one – the most effective one, a double door at the head of a short flight of steps – was strictly forbidden. The head porter, six foot six, in frock coat and brass buttons, was obdurate. 'This door cannot, it must not, it will not open.' Ours not to reason why; besides, there was no time for argument. The reason emerged next morning. I asked the man, who seemed a reasonable and friendly person, why he had been so firm. 'I will show you,' he said, and tiptoed down a veranda towards the double door. In the architrave was the nest of a pair of blue-tits; the little hen, nervous but gallant, fluttered about our heads. 'If this door had been used, she would have deserted her eggs; you wouldn't have wanted that.'

Tyrone Guthrie,
A Life in the Theatre, 1960, pp. 168, 170–1.

Tyrone Guthrie directs *Henry VIII* at Stratford-upon-Avon, 1949–50.

An incident, typical of Guthrie direction, occurred in the scene where Katharine of Aragon, in response to the threatened divorce, pleads her wounded case to the King. By Henry's choice this was made into a public, not a private scene, although she strove to keep it private between husband and wife. In the middle of her long speech, Henry started tapping a ruler on a table . . . rap . . . rap . . . rap. Quietly and slowly at first, while he beamed with an ever-so-winning expression of long-suffering boredom to his sycophantic court; then louder and more insistent, as she continued (in the face of ribald laughter) with a parallel growth of desperation. This 'rap-rap' not only served to make her speak louder and therefore unwittingly publicly; it also served to show the world that he, Henry, regarded her remarks as unworthy even of attention and that the world, including the Pope, had better take note. A seductive, private plea was ruthlessly made public, laughable and, in the end, painfully touching. The production was full of such inspirations.

Michael Langham, in Alfred Rossi,
Astonish Us in the Morning: Tyrone Guthrie Remembered, 1980, p. 284.

Henry VIII went on forever, because we did it two years running at Stratford, 1949 and 50. I was in both, played the same part. Then, when it was redone at the Old Vic for the Coronation, I played a different part.

And there happened an interesting thing. Tony [Guthrie] gave me the Lord Chamberlain, lots of comedy, another old man, a controlling role in the mechanics of the play. In an early rehearsal, Tony said to me, 'Going to change what we did before. Going to give you the Prologue and the Epilogue.' They had been done at Stratford by a very good elderly actress who was also 'inside' the play. And she came again to the Vic. He said, 'It would be much better if the Chamberlain had all that, and controlled the whole entertainment "inside" and "outside" the play at the same time. Can't think why I didn't do it before.' I said to him, 'She's not going to like that.' He said, 'No, no, no, we'll do it, there we are.' So the news was given to her, and she was terribly upset. And after a few rehearsals she really was extremely unhappy. And I went to Tony and I said, 'You know this is marvellous for me, and I'm enjoying it, but it's not going to work. She's miserable.' He said, 'It's my decision, we stick to it.' The poor woman was in tears at one time. I went to him again and said, 'Please, give it back to her.' And he said, 'Yes,

I think I'll have to. Think it's a pity. But till the end of this week you will do it. Question of discipline.'

I was absolutely fascinated by that. He'd agreed that he was going to give it back, the *status quo* of the previous production was going to be restored, *but* somebody had gone against his artistic decision; punishment must be administered. And, you see, without that kind of hard spine of discipline, I don't see how you can run a company.

Robert Hardy, in Alfred Rossi, *Astonish Us in the Morning: Tyrone Guthrie Remembered*, 1980, pp. 141–2.

Sir Laurence Olivier (Baron Olivier of Brighton)

Actor, 1902–1989

I got a job at one time with a troupe called the Lena Ashwell players. We used to play in swimming baths in Deptford, Ilford, Watford, Islington, Shadwell, paying our own fares – I was nearly starving getting £2.10s a week. We had to dress in the cubicles and sometimes in the lavatories, and so we became known as the Lavatory Players. Well, I had an opportunity with them when I was playing Flavius in *Julius Caesar*. There was a couple of very dreary wreaths pinned to the curtain, and the great thing to do was to tear them down angrily, and, if possible, tear down the curtain as well, to see the naked behinds of the girls dressing at the back; that was a big laugh. And one day Marullus was standing on a little beer box as a rostrum and saying, 'Knew you not Pompey,' and he had long pants and they came off underneath his toga and folded over his beer box so he couldn't move, couldn't get off. Well, I laughed so much I had to leave the stage; and the next morning I was fired.

Laurence Olivier, BBC interview, 1965.

Ralph Richardson advises Laurence Olivier on how to play Mercutio, 1935.

I hope that you are not very bored with all this my dear boy – but one thing more – the difficulty is to keep sober enough in the one hour twenty-five minutes wait you have before the end to take your call without falling into the orchestra-pit. This takes years of skill and cannot be overestimated, as much of the effect of the poetic 'Mab' speech may be lost by such an incident.

Ralph Richardson, letter to Laurence Olivier;
John Cottrell, *Laurence Olivier*, 1977, pp. 105–6.

Earlier in their careers, when Olivier couldn't learn the part of Iago, Richardson, who was playing Othello, told him: 'My dear fellow, I'm afraid you'll have to give up sex for four or five days.' Olivier said: 'What's that got to do with it?' And Richardson replied: 'Phosphates in the brain. You shot all yours, and it's phosphates that retain the memory.' Olivier recalled: 'I gave it up and in four days learned the part.'

Garry O'Connor,
The Sunday Times, 16 July 1989, p. C2.

Olivier plays Iago in Tyrone Guthrie's production of *Othello* at the Old Vic, 1938.

Anyway, I was influenced by the idea of playing it all for charm, an absolute charmer so that everyone would say 'honest Iago' with complete conviction. But actually I think it's quite wrong and I think that the NCO Iago is right. And Othello didn't have him because he wasn't the right man for the job, he wasn't sufficient for Othello, who needed support of class very much, being a blackamoor. You can call it what you like, you can call him Negro. We hear towards the end of the play that he came from Mauretania. Which was right on the *blackest* east coast of Africa. And some people have it that he's a Berber Moor. A blackamoor doesn't mean a Moorish Moor at all. A black man was a blackamoor. He was a *black* man. And all Shakespeare cared about was the idea of a black man strangling a white girl.

But we tried to justify Iago's evil by making it a psychological impulse, that he himself didn't understand, rather like Hamlet and the Oedipus complex, that absolutely subconsciously Iago was in love with Othello. And it couldn't work, because you couldn't express it. So there I was being a charming young blade with a beautiful undergraduate's accent and not making any sense at all. As far as I remember I was every bit as classy as Tony Quayle who played Cassio – so the only interpretation that makes sense is the NCO. And you can hear Othello saying, 'I don't think so. I think I'll have this young Florentine,' you know, with his splendid graces and airs and that. And Iago, like a gnarled NCO soldier, would hope to Christ he was going to get into the officer class and when he failed he was going to react like everybody I've seen in any service I've ever been in, which was only one, the Navy. And when you are in a service, you *understand* Iago.

When you're in the service you'll be eating and a hand will come over your shoulder and you look at the wrist and see how many stripes are on it before you look up. When you're in *that* sort of set-up and somebody is expecting an extra half-stripe and doesn't get it, you see him eating *into himself*, in the mess, you know. Absolutely white and grey with shame and betrayed hopes. And when somebody younger has got the half-stripe more than they, and they've just been shown once again that they're not quite the right class, to be a lieutenant commander, you know. I was ridden by one of these men, an NCO class man, who *did* get a half-stripe, and as soon as he got his half-stripe he'd start taking it out on me:

'How's our film star today?' All that sort of thing. And I let it get me down, and I really got into the fantasy class of hatred of this man and I used to walk about the aerodrome saying, 'How can I get him, how can I get him?' One day walking across the field, I stopped right in the middle of it and said, 'Of course, he's married. Christ, Iago!'

Laurence Olivier, in Alfred Rossi,
Astonish Us in the Morning: Tyrone Guthrie Remembered, 1980, pp. 98–9.

Olivier plays Richard III at the New Theatre, 1944.

Well, I'd been on the stage now for twenty years. I'd just finished *Henry V* and, I don't know how, or why, I just went into it with the same distrust of the critics, the same fear of public opinion as I had always experienced. I went on to the stage frightened, heart beating, came on, locked the door behind me, approached the footlights and started. And I – I just simply went through it. I don't think anybody in the company believed in the project at all. I think everybody was rather in despair about the whole production. And nobody particularly believed in my performance, none of us particularly believed in any of our performances; I don't think even our producer, John Burrell, believed in it much. In the first three plays which we presented, Ralph Richardson had brought *Peer Gynt* off brilliantly, *Arms and the Man* was a success on its own, and now there was this rather poor relation, with a part that people had seen quite a lot of. And so I didn't know – I didn't know; I was just once more going to have, as we say, a bash. I had developed this characterization, and I had got a lot of things on my side, now I come to think of it, from the point of view of timeliness. One had Hitler over the way, one was playing it definitely as a paranoic, so that there was a core of something to which the audience would immediately respond. I fancy, I may be quite wrong, but I fancy I possibly filled it out, possibly enriched it a bit with a little more humour than a lot of other people had done, but I'm not sure about that. I only know that I read a few notices, stayed up till three and drank a little too much.

My next performance was the next-day matinée, for which I was all too ill-prepared. But there was something in the atmosphere. There is a phrase – the sweet smell of success – and I can only tell you (I've had two experiences of that), it just smells like Brighton and oyster-bars and things like that. And as I went down to the prompt corner, darling Diana Boddington, my stage manager, and still one of our stage managers at the National, sort of held out her hand and said, 'It's marvellous, darling', or something like that, and I said, 'Oh, is it?', and as I went on to the stage – the house was not even full – I felt this thing. I felt for the first time that the critics had approved, that the public had approved, and they had created a kind of grapevine, and that particular audience had felt impelled to come to see me. It was an overwhelming feeling, a head-reeling feeling, and it went straight to my head. I felt the feeling I'd never felt before, this complete confidence. I felt, if you like, what an actor must finally feel: I felt a little power of hypnotism; I felt that I had them. It went to my head, as I said, to such an extent that I didn't even bother to put on the limp. I thought, I've got them anyway, I needn't bother with all this characterization any more. It's an awful story really.

Laurence Olivier,
Great Acting, ed. Hal Burton, 1967, pp. 24–5.

Olivier on the casting of his film *Hamlet*.

It was ancient custom for the most ancient actor-managers to play Hamlet; I am sure Irving was in his sixties before finishing with the part. I was on the cusp of forty. As one of my predecessors is reputed to have said in reply to the earnest question, 'Did Hamlet sleep with Ophelia?', 'In my company, always.' His mother Gertrude was probably the elderly character actress in his company – likely enough, his wife. My own arrangements were as different as could be. In 1947 Eileen Herlie, playing my mum, was thirteen years younger than I; it must be a record. I worried not at all whether I would get away with such a major imprudence. 'For goodness sake,' I said, 'it's *Hamlet*.'

Laurence Olivier,
Confessions of an Actor, 1982, p. 123.

Olivier tells how he developed his characterisation of Shylock (1970).

It started in front of the shaving mirror one morning after I knew I was going to play him and had read the play with that in mind. It would take me half an hour or more each day to shave because I would experiment with the way I went about it. I would discard my normal way of shaving and experiment with other ways, finding the way I would do it if I was Shylock. But it is not just the act of shaving – it's everything that goes with it, from how one holds one's hands on the razor to the facial expressions, grunts, sighs, and so on, that are involved in shaving. And how one positions one's head, how one stands and shifts one's weight. All of that, and soon you are shaving completely differently and that's your Shylock shaving.

Laurence Olivier, *Dick Cavett Show*, PBS, 1980.

Alec Clunes

Director, actor, manager, 1912–1970

Alec Clunes plays Benedick at Stratford-upon-Avon, 1939.

Alec Clunes . . . had shocking luck. At the end of the first act electric power failed over a large area in the Midlands. The interval drowsed on for half-an-hour. Then, in despair, a 'secondary system' was switched on, one that left the stage in what the West of England calls owl-light. The play was acted on the narrow forestage in front of the curtain; but it was a tedious business, and everybody, especially the artists, felt relieved when, after ninety minutes, the lights blossomed. Jay Laurier, the Dogberry, who had kept going untroubled, shook the house with a beatific smile at Borachio's appropriate line, 'What your wisdom could not discover, these shallow fools have brought to light.'

J. C. Trewin, *Alec Clunes*, 1958, p. 41.

•

There is a fine story about a prominent British Othello of this century who took an acting company into the provinces – a good company, with a particularly talented Iago to give the show balance. At the first stop, Iago drew all the rave reviews. The Moor promptly disengaged himself of this evil man, and for his next booking took a rather less competent Iago. This substitute also proved a villain and drew the best notices, and again the injured Moor rid himself of his crafty

Ancient. For the next stop, he protected himself by giving the Iago role to an untried stage hand. This time, when the reviews came out, all the critics' good words were still for the villain. The distinguished actor capitulated. He engaged the best Othello he could find, and took the part of Iago for himself, and basked in glowing notices for the rest of the tour.

Marvin Rosenberg,
The Masks of Othello, 1961, p. 141.

Sir Donald Wolfit

Actor-manager, 1902–1968

To his audience, undoubtedly, the moment outside the play to be enjoyed most, was his curtain call. No matter how long or short the part, Wolfit took his solo call with precisely the same degree of utter mental and physical exhaustion. He could be bellowing at an actor for ruining a scene just as he was due to step out before the audience; the moment his turn came, a blanket of weariness seemed to overcome him, and banging the curtain with his hand, he would slowly make his way, through the gap, into the light. There, he would hold on to the curtain with his right hand, bow low, his left hand cocked behind him. Peter Cotes continues the story:

> Before he actually spoke and the applause was at its loudest, he would slowly raise, as though with great effort, a frail and tired hand in an undemanding appeal for silence, the while a rather sickly, grateful smile appeared on his face (as though this was a tremendous effort, too). Obviously, this was a sacrosanct moment, the induction to a climax of almost religious intensity.

> After the struggle to remain upstanding with one hand on the curtain for support, DW divested himself of every bit of fatigue; he was martial as, with that well-known pose (Christ on his way to Calvary), he declaimed his thanks; the noble indignation rising, his eye, all bespoke the virtuous hero – a man alone up there on the stage, albeit warmed by his audience down there in the auditorium. By the time he had finished that speech, his face already running with sweat . . . he bowed his way back through the opening in the curtain.

. . . Norman Marshall observed the following scene in the foyer of the King's Theatre, Hammersmith: two old ladies who had seen Wolfit play Malvolio that afternoon, and had witnessed, of course, the curtain call, went round to the box office and cancelled their seats for the performance of *King Lear* that evening. They informed the box office manageress that, as they had come all the way from the country, they were deeply disappointed that Mr. Wolfit was not to play Lear that night. The manageress replied that, as far as she knew, Mr. Wolfit had every intention of appearing. The two old ladies said that they doubted it, since he looked far too ill as he took his curtain calls.

Ronald Harwood,
Sir Donald Wolfit, C.B.E.: his life and work in the unfashionable theatre, 1971, pp. 245–6.

Wolfit omitted the scene where Malvolio is imprisoned and visited by Feste pretending to be Sir Topas. The actor contended that the scene was the work of another pen. 'I cannot learn it,' he declared, 'and if I cannot learn it, Shakespeare did not write it!'

Ronald Harwood,
Sir Donald Wolfit, C.B.E.: his life and work in the unfashionable theatre, 1971, p. 155.

. . . an ambitious but not overtalented young actor . . . was employed in Sir Donald Wolfit's travelling Shakespeare Company. His contribution to *Macbeth* was as the final messenger who has to run on stage and stammer out, 'My Lord, the queen is dead,' and then run away. For many seasons he did just this, and then he became bored and asked Sir Donald if he could play a larger part. Wolfit refused. The young actor continued to ask and Wolfit continued to refuse. The young actor became increasingly depressed and the matter developed into an obsession. Thoughts of revenge filled his waking hours and one evening he decided to sabotage the play. That night he ran onto the stage. 'My Lord,' he shouted, 'the queen is *much better and is even now at dinner*.' He then ran off, leaving the astonished actor-manager to deal with the situation as best he could.

Richard Huggett,
Supernatural on Stage: Ghosts and Superstitions of the Theatre, 1975, p. 211.

Wolfit's *Caesar*, in contrast to the Welles and Cass productions, was in style less modern-dress than fancy-dress. Or as he put it in a programme note, 'The uniforms are of no particular state or country but chosen for their colour value as applicable to the main characters.' Mystified reviewers and audiences speculated fruitlessly upon the relevance of each costume's cut and colour to its wearer; and Wolfit was chary of enlightenment . . . A decade later Alan Dent revealed (*News Chronicle*, 12 August 1960) that a query about the appropriateness of the uniforms prompted a letter from the company's wardrobe-mistress 'to explain that the real reason for the modern dress was that modern laundries – in immediate post-war conditions – refused to wash togas.' But the curious colour-scheme apparently went unexplained.

John Ripley,
'Julius Caesar' on stage in England and America 1599–1973, 1980, pp. 244–5.

•

When I said I was planning to do *Macbeth* [Alexander] Woollcott told me that the Lunts had always wanted to produce the play. 'Lynn has a wonderful idea,' he said. 'She will go naked to murder Duncan.' I agreed this would be a sensational effect, but how did she propose to do it? 'Oh,' said Woollcott, 'there will be a very high parapet between her and the audience; she will keep her pudenda strictly for Alfred.'

John Gielgud, *An Actor and his Time*, 1981, p. 175.

When Godfrey [Tearle] was playing the role [Antony] in New York, with Katharine Cornell as his Cleopatra, they made a great romantic entrance at the start of the play. Cleopatra spoke her first lines, 'If it be love, indeed, tell me how much,' and Godfrey came rushing on to the stage carrying her in his arms.

When the first night was over he said to her,

'I've been thinking. Perhaps we'd better walk on instead.'

'Oh Godfrey! But why?'

'Because I'm too old and you're too heavy.'

Jill Bennett and Suzanne Goodwin,
Godfrey: A Special Time Remembered, 1983, p. 141.

Peter Brook

Director, 1925–

Sir Barry Jackson took over the running of the Shakespeare Memorial Theatre, Stratford-upon-Avon, in 1946. He and the young Peter Brook went down from Birmingham to Stratford, to inspect the theatre:

Jackson announced that he was going down to Stratford to look over the Memorial the next day, and asked if Brook would like to accompany him. Flattered and excited, Brook agreed. The visit was, however, something of a shock. The two men found a building in which the ravages of wear and war had gone unchecked. Elizabeth Scott's modernist palace had weathered the last thirteen years badly. It had become a theatrical Satis House, a place where time had stood still, and where decay had been allowed to take its course. With mounting depression Brook tramped round an auditorium with torn carpets, sagging seats; a stage hung with filthy tabs, much of its machinery damaged and unrepaired. Backstage they found a now badly out-dated switchboard, no Tannoy, a litter of unclassified scenery, and everywhere hampers of musty smelling costumes. The theatre that had been hailed as one of the most advanced in Europe had fallen on hard times.

The urbane Sir Barry, to Brook's amazement, surveyed it all with equanimity. He gave the younger director a sharp glance, smiled, and lit a cigarette in his long holder. 'Oh yes,' he said finally, 'I think we could turn this into another Salzburg, don't you?'

Sally Beauman,
The Royal Shakespeare Company: A History of Ten Decades, 1982, pp. 166–7.

When Sir Barry Jackson asked me to direct *Love's Labour's Lost* in Stratford in 1946, it was my first big production and I had already done enough work in smaller theatres to know that actors, and above all stage managers, had the greatest contempt for anyone who, as they always put it, 'did not know what he wanted.' So the night before the first rehearsal I sat agonized in front of a model of the set, aware that further hesitation would soon be fatal, fingering folded pieces of cardboard – forty pieces representing the forty actors to whom the following morning I would have to give orders, definite and clear. Again and again, I staged the very first entry of the Court, recognizing that this was when all would be lost or won, numbering the figures, drawing charts, manoeuvring the scraps of cardboard to and fro, on and off the set, trying them in big batches, then in small, from the side, from the back, over grass mounds, down steps, knocking them all over with my sleeve, cursing and starting again. As I did so, I noted the moves, and with no one to notice my indecision, crossed them out, then made fresh notes. The next morning I arrived at rehearsal, a fat prompt-book under my arm, and the stage management brought me a table, reacting to my volume, I observed, with respect.

I divided the cast into groups, gave them numbers and sent them to their starting places, then, reading out my orders in a loud confident way, I let loose the first stage of the mass entrance. As the actors began to move I knew it was no good. These were not remotely like my cardboard figures, these large human beings thrusting themselves forward, some too fast with lively steps I had not foreseen, bringing them suddenly on top of me – not stopping, but wanting to go on, staring me in the face, or else lingering, pausing, even turning back with elegant affectations that took me by surprise. We had only done the first stage of the movement, letter A on my chart, but already everyone was wrongly placed and movement B could not follow. My heart sank and, despite all my preparation, I felt quite lost. Was I to start again, drilling these actors so that they conformed to my notes? One inner voice prompted me to do so, but another pointed out that my pattern was much less interesting than this new pattern that was unfolding in front of me – rich in energy, full of personal variations, shaped by individual enthusiasms and lazinesses, promising such different rhythms, opening so many unexpected possibilities. It was a moment of panic. I think, looking back, that my whole future work hung in the balance. I stopped, and walked away from my book, in amongst the actors, and I have never looked at a written plan since. I recognized once and for all the presumption and the folly of thinking that an inanimate model can stand for a man.

Peter Brook, *The Empty Space*, 1972, pp. 119–20.

Peter Brook follows Beerbohm Tree.

The casual proposal of an earlier rehearsal that a real animal should be introduced into 'the wood' of Act Three (made of wire and gantries), is now met by a grey rabbit. It is set down, with something close to a simper, by one of the more tender-hearted fairies. Nose twitching, it faces the clownish onrush of Quince, Bottom and the others for only a moment . . . and then bolts for it, tail bobbing. Its custodian must recover it. He revolts, aghast and pouting. He will not do it. He is in a pet over it, indignant and sulking. He will not, he says to Brook, 'submit him to these frights'. There is oafish laughter from the other actors. 'His terrors,' he announces, mouth puckering and near to stamping his foot, 'were not funny.' Arms akimbo, the mechanicals bellow at these fairy flounces. But it is the end of Brook's rabbit. 'Are we all met?' asks Bottom, subsiding. 'Pat, pat,' says Quince, as off-stage the rabbit is noisily recaptured.

David Selbourne,
The Making of 'A Midsummer Night's Dream',
1982, pp. 256–7.

Claire Bloom

Actress, 1931–

Hamlet at Stratford-upon-Avon, 1948.

I came to the first rehearsal to play Ophelia, having read every footnote in the Variorum, and every book on *Hamlet* I could find. I was seventeen, Ophelia surely little more. The part seemed easily within my grasp: to love desperately, to be rejected, to go mad, and to die. I think Benthall was amused by the amount of homework I had done and let me go about working the part out for myself. I remember that I couldn't find a way to begin the mad scene, couldn't connect it to anything real to me. I knew the shock of her father's death must have fallen like a wall between Ophelia and everything around her, but I had no idea how to demonstrate the magnitude of her displacement. In the third week of rehearsal I went into a shop and a woman, obviously mentally disturbed, came in, and pointing to something, said, 'I want – I want – I want . . .' but was unable to complete the sentence. 'Where – where – where is the beauteous majesty of Denmark?' – and all at once I established for myself just how damaged was Ophelia's sense of time, place, and order.

Claire Bloom, *Limelight and After*, 1982, p. 71.

Diana Wynyard

Actress, 1906–1964

Diana Wynyard played Lady Macbeth at Stratford in 1948 with Sir Godfrey Tearle's Macbeth and directed by Michael Benthall. She didn't believe in the curse and made the sad mistake of saying so shortly after the dress rehearsal. Just before she went on for the sleep-walking scene, she decided that the way she had been rehearsing it, and the traditional way of playing it, was all wrong. Sleepwalkers did *not* walk with their eyes open, as they had always been shown. They walked with their eyes *shut*, and without telling anybody she went on the stage on the first night and put the theory into practice. The rostrum was wide enough for comfort, and, as she had been rehearsing it for several days, she thought she knew exactly how far it went and at what point it started to curve round. The first-night audience gasped audibly with horror as she slipped from the rostrum and fell fifteen feet. It was a mark of her professionalism that she picked herself up and continued with the scene, and of her courage that, although bruised, bandaged, and considerably shaken, she did not miss any performances.

Richard Huggett,
Supernatural on Stage: Ghosts and Superstitions of the Theatre, 1975, p. 180.

•

Nevill Coghill directs a famous *Tempest* at Worcester College gardens, Oxford, in 1949.

To finish *The Tempest*, Nevill wanted the repaired ship to dock at the water's edge – in this case the shore of Worcester lake nearest the audience – and for Prospero, having said farewell to his island, Caliban, and Ariel, to embark with the court and, as he sailed away, really to drown his book, full fathom five. Ariel would trip across the water in five balletic leaps, on a board which had been constructed to reach out about twenty yards into the middle of the lake. This line of duckboards was built two inches under the water level, and made it look as if I was walking on the water itself.

As Prospero reminded us that his 'ending was despair/ Unless it be relieved by prayer', the huge vessel (a series of punts lashed together and surmounted by the replica of a Venetian sailing ship) was punted into position by the sailors, Prospero set Ariel free, and bade farewell to Caliban who dropped back into the water whence he had originally crawled. Here, at the lake's edge, close to the bank, a galvanized iron tub had been placed into which Caliban could fall, and hide himself from the audience, who believed him to have gone into the water. (During rehearsals, children being shown round the garden used to come over to him for a chat.)

As the boat sailed away into the darkness, lit by a single spot, I was to leap out across the lake, stop and blow kisses to Prospero and his friends in the boat, then turn and run back over the submerged boards until I reached the shore again; then towards the trees at the back of the lake, still waving to the boat. In those trees Nevill had built a ramp which enabled me to run right up until I seemed to be standing above the highest branches. Once steadied at the top, I was to turn and spread my arms, as though appealing to the heavens, and there beneath me a flare exploded, and every light in the auditorium and across the lake went out, as though dowsed by the magic of Ariel himself. It was superb, a set-piece which has been etched into the memory of our Oxford generation.

Charles Hodgson, quoted by Humphrey Carpenter, *OUDS: A Centenary History of the Oxford University Dramatic Society 1885–1985*, 1985, pp. 161–2.

We had an American Caliban. Nevill had his own good reasons for this piece of casting, which threw character into relief in an amazing way, although the idea originally raised a few eyebrows. His exploration of the text was most revealing of all. This Caliban had I suppose one of the most original entrances ever given to the character. He emerged bodily from the lake, where he had laid concealed long before the assembly of the audience, in a waterproof tank.

John Schlesinger, 'Oxford Theatricals, 1948', in *To Nevill Coghill From Friends*, Collected by John Lawlor and W. H. Auden, 1966, p. 101.

Sir Alec Guinness

Actor, 1914–

Alec Guinness plays Hamlet at the New Theatre, 1951.

There was booing on the first night and we got a bad press. But the second performance found the audience extremely receptive. Alec took his curtain call holding the worst of the notices behind his back. As applause mounted he stepped forward and proceeded to quote them. The audience commented with strenuous denials. When he'd finished he produced and read from the American publication *Shakespeare for the Masses*, a comic strip version of *Hamlet*. The audience rocked with laughter, then rose and gave Alec a standing ovation. It was a triumph. 'He's a game 'un,' remarked his Gravedigger, Stanley Holloway. He was indeed.

Patrick Crean,
More Champagne Darling, 1981, p. 250.

Whim, not will, is his ruler. He is in many ways the most impetuous, least premeditated of actors. At one performance of *Hamlet*, stung by the unwonted brusqueness with which Rosencrantz delivered the line: 'My lord, you must tell us where the body is and go with us to the king', he obeyed instinct, strode the width of the stage, smiling glassily, and slapped the offender hard across the ear, almost knocking him into the orchestra pit. It was a purely automatic reaction. Afterwards, in the wings, he swarmed up to the bruised victim (who jumped nervously) and: 'I'm so sorry,' he said, his eyes moist with apology, 'but you were so *insolent*, I felt I had to.'

Kenneth Tynan, *Alec Guinness*, 1953, p. 92.

His visual sense is not his strongest point, and it was at its most erratic in the climax of the play-scene, when he suddenly decided to indulge in a little expressionism. This took place just after I had taken leave of the Player Queen and dropped off to sleep. As the murderer crept up to slip me the potion, there was a slow black-out, except for a single spotlight on Claudius' face. Phosphorescent paint had been applied to the crown, the vial of poison and a great plastic left ear which I wore over my own: these glowed in the darkness, and the tableau as the poison was poured took on the aspect of an advertisement for a proprietary brand of rum. As an idea, provocative; but in execution, comic. It was cut out after the first performance. I remember handing over the ear to the stage manager, and feeling, for a moment, remarkably like Van Gogh.

Kenneth Tynan, *Alec Guinness*, 1953, p. 79.

Franco Zeffirelli

Director and designer, 1923–

February, 1967: the playwright Joe Orton, with his companion Kenneth Halliwell, was in the audience for Zeffirelli's production of *Much Ado About Nothing*.

Last night Kenneth and I watched, with increasing aggravation, Zeffirelli's National Theatre production of Shakespeare's *Much Ado About Nothing*. Maggie Smith as Beatrice. Robert Stephens as Benedick. Dressed early twentieth century and set (one supposes) in Sicily. This to be guessed at since most of the settings were composed of tulle rosebushes, draperies and irrelevant bits of architecture. Living statues looking like some set-piece in a pre-war follies. Occasionally they came to life and winked or even shook hands with the characters. Most of the cast had Italian accents except Beatrice and Benedick. Dogberry and the watch had such ludicrous accents that of course, all the malapropisms were lost. The play mangled, the verse butchered. The cold, calculated line of Don John, 'Your Hero, My Hero, any man's Hero,' ended in Don John sticking out his tongue. 'Sigh No More Ladies' – sung by a fat queeny ice-cream vendor – was camped unmercifully. The play disappeared under a welter of tricks. God's curse light upon all directors!

Ed. John Lahr, *The Orton Diaries*, 1986, p 80.

•

Orson Welles plays Othello at the St James's Theatre, 1951.

He discussed the production, and especially his interpretation of the title role, with Laurence Olivier first, and Olivier 'implored me to commit suicide by bringing out a small, curved knife and cutting myself from ear to ear,' says Orson. 'I thought it was a very bad idea – and he went ahead and did it years later.' Welles had his own advice for Olivier: he says that he suggested to Olivier that he would make a great Iago, to which Olivier instantly replied 'Why not Othello?' 'Because to play Othello you need a bass voice,' said Orson. At this Olivier's eyes lowered, and the discussion ended. According to Orson, Olivier then went to a voice coach, who, by the time Olivier appeared in *Othello* in 1964, had made him sound rather like James Earl Jones.

Barbara Leaming, *Orson Welles*, 1985, p. 383.

In the same production of *Othello*, Peter Finch played Iago.

Finchie maintained the *Othello* production was a traumatic crash course in an amazing larger-than-life experience. First of all Olivier came to see the production before it opened in London, and ticked off Peter for the dying inflectional fall at the end of every line that was taking all the meaning out of Shakespeare's poetry. 'You've got a good diaphragm,' Larry told him. 'Learn to use it like an opera singer when you play Shakespeare or else the poetry starts to sag with a lot of unnecessary pauses for breath.' Off went Finchie, and a week later his voice was rising beautifully like a castrato's at the end of every line of the bard's iambic pentameters. However, one night Noël Coward, by then a friend of Peter's, arrived at the dressing room after the performance and told Finchie's dresser, 'Pour the master a VERY large gin because I'm going to be naughty.' As Finchie entered he was greeted by Noël. 'It's an impeccable performance, Finchetta dear boy,' and then after an immaculately timed pause, 'but why are we playing Iago in Welsh?'

Trader Faulkner,
Peter Finch: A Biography, 1979, p. 145.

In November 1951, at the small Irving Theatre near Leicester Square, Ken [Tynan] co-directed with Ellen Pollock a programme of Grand Guignol of which the centrepiece was an abridged version – cut by Ken and Peter Myers – of *Titus Andronicus*. The presence of the St John Ambulance men, Ken assured his critics, was not superfluous attention-getting. 'An average of two people, in an audience of just over a hundred, have fainted at each performance. And last Sunday, to everyone's astonishment, one of the Ambulance men fainted himself.'

Kathleen Tynan,
The Life of Kenneth Tynan, 1987, p. 96.

One actor arrived at Stratford after rehearsals of *Richard III* had begun . . . [in 1953] . . . this actor was to play the corpse of my father-in-law. Glen [Byam Shaw] did not want a dummy corpse, he wanted an actor. At his first rehearsal, the actor lay on the bier, and during an interchange between Marius Goring as Richard, and myself, Glen stopped the rehearsal, and said earnestly to the corpse, 'This is a three-handed scene between Richard, the Lady Anne, and you.' The corpse was so surprised that he sat bolt upright.

It seems in fact rather chi-chi to expect that a scene will have any different effect if played by a dummy corpse or an actor acting a corpse, but in practice I discovered to my amazement that Glen was right. On the nights when the corpse hurried into the bier at the last moment, and gave no feeling except that of being bloody uncomfortable, I did not weep over him as I was able to on the nights when he lay seemingly sad and dead.

Yvonne Mitchell, *Actress*, 1957, pp. 90–1.

Richard Burton

Actor, 1925–1984

Burton plays Hamlet at the Old Vic, 1953.

His Hamlet on the whole was well received. He was 'moody, virile and baleful', he had 'dash, attack and verve'. John Gielgud did not like it much. After he had seen it he came around to Richard's dressing room to take him to dinner, and observing he was beset by visitors, said,'Shall I go ahead or wait until you're better – I mean, ready?' Burton loved to re-tell that story. Winston Churchill came and is said to have sat in the front stalls and muttered the lines along with the Prince and when he came backstage, requested, 'My Lord Hamlet, may I use your facilities?' That too was retailed. As was the story of two of the supporting cast who were supposed to lower a flag over Hamlet during his final dying monologue. Stage discipline had been getting slack – Burton, for instance, had imitated Gielgud throughout one performance – and Michael Benthall, the director, had issued severe warnings. As the flag was being lowered, the house hushed and the dark and tragic Prince of Denmark was uttering his last words, Burton the Prince looked to one of those two rather camp gentlemen who murmured out of the side of his mouth: 'So who's the boy in black?' He loved the stories as much as the acting.

Melvyn Bragg,
RICH: The Life of Richard Burton, 1988, pp. 95–6.

In *King John* he played the Bastard. George Devine, the director, had the idea of leaving Burton on stage throughout as a 'Chorus'. This had to be abandoned, as Philip Burton happily recorded, because 'Nobody could take their eyes off Richard.' Silent and stuck at the side of the stage with the best of British classical actors about him, he would still demand the audience's full attention.

Melvyn Bragg,
RICH: The Life of Richard Burton, 1988, p. 97.

Burton plays Hamlet on Broadway, 1964.

Following the performance . . . Richard Burton returned to his Regency Hotel suite and told Mrs Burton that he had been booed. Mrs Burton was watching television at the time and said, 'So what?' Mr Burton became agitated and asked her to turn off the television. 'Do you understand, my darling, that I have been booed? I played Hamlet tonight and I was *booed*!' Mrs Burton – being a woman who does not take an individual opinion seriously unless she knows the individual – could not understand her husband's arousal and was reluctant to turn off the program. Mr Burton then kicked at the screen of the set with sufficient force to shatter the picture tube. Since he was not wearing shoes, he wounded his foot so badly that a physician had to be summoned. A number of stitches were inserted between the first two toes.

Burton arrived at the theatre on the following evening with a decided limp. He insisted on playing the performance with the limp and said, 'Some critics have said I play Hamlet like Richard the Third anyway, so what the hell is the difference?'

William Redfield,
Letters from an Actor, New York, 1967, p. 238–9.

•

As Lady Macbeth, Vivien Leigh had certain shortcomings; but the intensity of her scenes with Olivier, then her husband in fact as well as in the play, was one of the elements that made Glen Byam Shaw's 1955 production at Stratford an outstanding experience. Yet two eminent Shakespearean scholars, who had made major contributions not only to textual studies but as expositors of the import of Shakespeare's plays, could agree, as they sat together in the stalls waiting for the play to restart after the interval, that they preferred not to see Shakespeare acted. Though their confession shocked me, it would not at that time have seemed particularly strange or reprehensible to the majority of academics. Twenty years later the climate has changed, at least superficially.

Richard David,
Shakespeare in the Theatre, 1978, p. 1.

I remember once discussing the part with Anthony Quayle, when we were both in *Titus Andronicus* behind the Iron Curtain. He had asked me if I was finding Titus tough going. 'It has', he said, 'all the hallmarks of a tough part.' 'Oh, God, yes,' I replied, 'but I suppose Macbeth is the worst, isn't it?' To which Quayle replied: 'No. Macbeth is positive, he knows what he is doing and he does it. He is a much jollier part altogether for the actor. Everybody flogs you every time they look at you as Titus. You are bemoaning your fate throughout and whatever happens to you is just another ghastly stroke of the knout, making you wail, "Oh, oh, oh, that this should happen to me." Othello's another part that's entirely composed of moaning, bellowing and screaming against fate. Macbeth is much more fun!' A sentiment I would agree with.

Laurence Olivier, *On Acting*, 1986, p. 75.

John Houseman directs *King John* at Stratford, Connecticut, in 1956.

Rouben Ter-Arutunian, besides designing the new Festival Stage and the scenery for our first two productions, was also responsible for our costumes. To convey the archaic, historical tone of the play, it had been agreed that the actors in *King John* should have an oversized, 'epic' appearance. Rouben fulfilled the assignment and went beyond it. The costumes he designed, particularly those of the military figures, were not only 'epic'; they were gigantic.

For economic and practical reasons we had decided against real chain mail. In its place our warriors were encased in padded, oversized suits of armour made up of brightly painted plaques of wood, plastic and synthetic rubber. These were handsome to look at but so bulky that when the actors inside them attempted to move they suggested the inflated figure of the Michelin Man. Besides, they became so costly that they were issued only to kings, nobles and military leaders. For the rest, Rouben raided half the Army and Navy surplus stores in New York and came out with a collection of pea jackets, padded vests, life jackets and rubber rafts which, when cut up and sewn back together into medieval uniforms, delighted him with their formidable mass.

All martial figures were supposed to wear tall leather hip boots. Since these too were far beyond our resources, only the élite received them. The lower ranks were supplied with huge grey-green rubber waders (acquired in stores specialising in fishing equipment) which rose all the way to the crotch and which proved almost impossible to work in on account of their volume and weight but even more because of the fiendish heat generated in their airless depths when the stage lights hit them.

On the day of our dress parade the temperature at Stratford was close to 90 degrees at noon and had gone down only slightly by midafternoon when the company arrived at the theatre and began putting on its costumes. From where I sat in the house I became aware of some grumbling rising from the dressing rooms below, which increased as the frailer members of the cast struggled to drag themselves and their boots up the steep steps that led to the stage.

Instead of the usual dress parade, I had decided, for lack of time, on a 'run-through' in costume. Early in the first act an apprentice, a stripling in his teens, suddenly collapsed. With all that rubberised material on him he made a strange soft slurping thud as he fell. Peter Zeisler, our production stage manager, appeared from backstage with an assistant and dragged him off while the run-through continued. Rouben was seated beside me taking costume notes; I gave him a questioning look, to which he responded with a shrug. The gravity of our situation was not yet apparent.

Halfway through rehearsal, with the embattled forces of France and England confronting each other while Jean Rosenthal checked and adjusted her light cues, that ghastly slurping thud was heard again and then repeated with increasing frequency as, one after another, singly and in pairs, the warriors of both armies began to collapse. After the seventh had gone down I glanced at Rouben. While he muttered 'Amateurs' and 'Sabotage', another keeled over and then another and another. Before long there were twelve dehydrated bodies (five nobles and seven soldiers) lying on our new shining platform – some out cold, others still conscious and writhing as they struggled to tear off their boots and jackets.

I called off rehearsal and gave the actors a two-hour dinner break. When they returned from their long dinner they found that their boots and jackets had been punched, pierced, gouged and lacerated to permit the passage of air and the removal of several hundred pounds of cotton padding. During the next few days many additional rents and punctures appeared – most of them made by the actors themselves. By the time we opened, our soldiers had a ragged, thoroughly 'medieval' and 'epic' appearance and the fainting rate was down to one or two a week.

John Houseman,
Unfinished Business, 1986, pp. 356–7.

As Lovel, in *Richard III* at Stratford, I surpassed myself one evening. I dried. I couldn't remember the two lines:

> Here is the head of that ignoble traitor,
> The dangerous and unsuspected Hastings.

Christopher Plummer, playing Richard, waited and waited for me to speak. Then he pointed at the head I was holding and inquired:

> Is that the head of that ignoble traitor,
> The dangerous and unsuspected Hastings?

To which Lovel, nodding vigorously, replied 'Yes.'

Paul Bailey,
My Drama School, ed. Margaret McCall, 1978, p. 167.

In 1963, faintly to her own surprise, Penelope Keith got into the Royal Shakespeare Company at Stratford:

> 'Spears, mainly, and crowd scenes in *Julius Caesar*. John Blatchley, the director, said we were all to be real people and say things, so on the first night just as Mark Antony started the speech I said "Have an ear" and just then everyone in the crowd fell silent and the whole audience heard me and Bernard Levin was jolly rude about me in his notice the next morning. I thought of drowning myself in the Avon but when I went back on the second night the whole green room stood up and cheered because they said nobody in the crowd had ever got a Bernard Levin notice before.'*

Penelope Keith, *Profile* (Sheridan Morley),
The Times, 14 July 1976.

*In fact, the reviewer was Kenneth Tynan. 'By way of further deflation, a cackling hag greets the opening lines of "Friends, Romans, countrymen" with the derisive offer: "Here, have an ear!"' *The Observer, 14 April 1963.*

Alec Guinness and Simone Signoret play Macbeth and Lady Macbeth at the Royal Court Theatre, 1966.

Simone was wonderful to work with in a quite different way. She was deeply emotional with very little stage technique but at her best she was more immediately real than Alec. She would seize him in her capacious hands when she said, 'Oo woz eet zat zus cried?' and shake him. Alec begged her not to do it so brutally. After one performance he went to her dressing room and pulled up his sleeve revealing an ugly purple bruise. 'Oh, Alec, I'm so sorry.' Guinness took a cloth and wiped off the mark. He had concocted it with grease-paint. Their relationship was strong but they were not in the end the best of partners. The production opened to the most horrendous notices ever, or so it seemed. On the second night Simone's nerve went and she dried. Alec took her and held her till she nodded, said, 'OK,' and went on with the show.

William Gaskill, *A Sense of Direction*, 1988, p. 80.

Simone Signoret gives an interestingly varied account of the same episode.

On the third evening the last reviews had fallen before mine eyes – or rather on my head – just before I went onstage. There wasn't a reason in the world, I thought, that everyone in the audience hadn't read them too. And so it happened that during my first scene with Alec Guinness, during my third or fourth speech, I suddenly stopped. He caught on and saved me. He slid in, 'If we should fail . . .' which comes much later in the scene. He used it to save his friend, who was in the process of drowning, having 'dried up.' It helped me to go on, and since we were playing to an audience of connoisseurs, they applauded. When the time came for him to repeat 'If we should fail,' this time in context, they applauded again.

Simone Signoret,
Nostalgia isn't what it used to be, 1978, pp. 338–9.

Richard Eyre, Artistic Director, Royal National Theatre, tells of early experiences as an actor.

The first of these was *Henry V* at Hornchurch rep where, amongst many other experiences, I played Mountjoy the French Herald, in a costume that made me look like a rather worn playing-card. On my first entrance I faced a somewhat depleted but impish looking English army. I spoke my first line: 'You know me by my habit,' only to be greeted by barely concealed gestures of self-abuse under the knitted chain mail. Later in the evening I doubled as a member of both the French and the English armies, who ran frequently across the stage stopping only to fire arrows which bounced off the wall of the theatre to return forlornly to the foot of the archer, who picked it up, ran offstage, changed a helmet, and returned in the other direction to repeat the process as the opposing army. I still smart with shame when I think of it and of the audience who endured it without criminally assaulting the actors and the management of the theatre.

Richard Eyre,
The Hamlyn Lecture, July 1991.

Trevor Nunn

Director, 1940–

Julius Caesar at Stratford-upon-Avon, 1972.

Julius Caesar, rehearsed in the evening, after a break for supper, emerged cooler, more reflective and deliberate, gaining a stillness and economy from our tiredness after the day's exertions. One night we rehearsed the conspiracy scene in total darkness. The sense of danger, furtiveness and fright was extraordinary. On another, there was a long, disturbingly messy improvisation of Caesar's murder, Mark Dignam taking what seemed hours to die, after which everyone had to describe their reactions. The Senate guards, who had stood rooted to their posts throughout, had an odd but convincing explanation of their inertia – none of them dared interrupt such famous, excited statesmen arguing over the dictator's body with waving, bloody arms.

Trevor Nunn, in 'Writing on Sand',
Theatre 73, ed. Sheridan Morley, 1973, p. 57.

•

Michael Hordern seeks help from Gielgud.

I asked him if he had any advice to help one get through the run. 'Yes,' he said, 'get a small Cordelia.'

The Times, 29 May 1969.

Peter Hall

Director, 1930–

Tuesday, 4 July 1972

I rode home with Larry [Olivier] from a meeting at Max Rayne's and talked about *The Tempest* as the one play I wanted to do and the need for him to play Prospero. I pointed out that Prospero was acted traditionally by a remote old man – an aesthetic schoolmaster who was thinking of higher things, whereas Prospero should really be a man of power, of intelligence, as shrewd and cunning and egocentric as Churchill.

Larry listened. I think he was interested. He said he wanted to play the part for comedy, and that Prospero should lecture his daughter in the first scene while shaving. He said he couldn't wear all those whiskers and wigs Prosperos always wore. I love the fact that actors always go straight to their appearance. When Bully Bottom is given the part of Pyramus in *A Midsummer Night's Dream*, the first question he asks director Quince is: 'What beard were I best play it in?' There speaks the actor.

Peter Hall, *Peter Hall's Diaries*,
ed. John Goodwin, 1983, p. 12.

Hamlet at the National Theatre, 1975–6.

Wednesday, 26 November 1975

Tense atmosphere at *Hamlet* rehearsal this morning. Poor Angela Lansbury has to leave tomorrow for three days in Los Angeles as her mother has died in Hollywood. Our rhythm of work disturbed. I tidied up a few things, and then we went into the run-through. It was not bad, slightly jumpy, slightly crude, things which had long been secure going awry, Angela obviously working under great strain. She came on for the Ophelia's death news and started the 'One woe doth tread upon another's heels so fast they follow . . .' speech with the most amazing emotional complexity. Then she stopped; nearly went on; tried to control herself; tried to go on. The silence lasted for ever. Denis Quilley collected her into his arms. Her grief was too much. An extraordinary moment. Everyone in the cast felt the reality of death – and the second half of *Hamlet* particularly is about death.

Peter Hall, *Peter Hall's Diaries*, 1983, p. 195.

Albert Finney plays Hamlet at the National Theatre, 1975–6.

Friday, 19 December 1975

Interesting point. He told me he'd had great difficulty in playing the last part of *Hamlet* because of his long time off stage. He would come off after 'How all occasions', have a Guinness, relax, and even have a little sleep. But when he at last came back to do the graveyard scene he couldn't get himself going again. He said that now he was adopting a different technique. On coming off he jumped into the shower and while soaping himself vigorously thought of the fight with the pirates and all the activity that was crowding in on the life of Hamlet. He then didn't relax but came on again as keyed up as possible. He said he loved playing the part so much he resented this long gap when he was off stage.

Peter Hall, *Peter Hall's Diaries*, 1983, p. 200.

Simon Callow

Director, actor, writer, 1949–

John Dexter directs *As You Like It* at the National Theatre, 1979.

For John, the rehearsal room is a garage, and he's the mechanic. Sweating and with oil on his hands, he assembles the components. The trick is to get the right components, and put them together in the right way. It's almost like a jigsaw puzzle. For some cars, there exist plans which are known to be reliable; for others, you have to work it out all on your own. As cars, so plays, for John. He's the best play-mechanic in the world. Not that he isn't eager for the actor's contribution. Nothing pleases him more in the world than an unsolicited piece of business. But – 'Don't describe it, DO it'. I never satisfied him more than the day we were rehearsing the dreaded Sonnet that Orlando pins to the tree for Rosalind. I said, 'It seems to call for a physical expression of his love, John.' 'Don't talk about it –' 'Do it, I know. OK.' 'O Rosalind,' I cried, and did a cartwheel. 'MARVELLOUS,' he shouted and *ran* onto the stage to edit it. 'At last,' he said, 'you're inventing.' I was actually copying. I'd been at his behest to the Chinese Acrobats, and this was my (rather modest) tribute to their work. The scene had been a stumbling block for me ever since the first day we'd rehearsed it, when John – this is very typical – had said 'I got hold of a copy of the film of *As You* that Larry made with Elisabeth Bergner. He did something absolutely extraordinary with this speech.' 'What?' 'I'm not going to tell you. Just do something equally extraordinary, that's all.' I don't know whether the cartwheel was that, but it pleased John no end.

Simon Callow, *Being An Actor*, 1984, p. 89.

•

As You Like It at Stratford-upon-Avon (Royal Shakespeare Company, 1980).

The wrestling scene was vital to the production and to my character [Orlando]. Losing weight and visiting a gym three times a week paid dividends. Ian McKay was the fight arranger. I had worked with him before, which meant he knew my limitations. Terry Wood was a marvellous Charles, the wrestler – six feet five inches and approximately twenty stone. I have nightmares about facing lunatic actors in stage fights, but Terry Wood dispelled my fears and I hope I did the same for him. Right from the start there was total trust, always the emphasis was on taking care of each other, and as a result of all this Ian was able to devise a fight that was both spectacularly entertaining and apparently dangerous; so much more difficult to do in unarmed combat than it is with weapons. This proved to be essential to the production. In keeping with the fairy tale idea we had a fight that was reminiscent of professional wrestling at the local town hall between opponents grossly mismatched. It had moments of hilarity mixed with moments of alarming brutality. It was generally at this point that audiences loosened up and sometimes joined in. There were often boos, cheers and rounds of applause. At my suggestion we incorporated a move in which I was hurled headlong into the front row of the audience. This often took me out of the vision of the upper circles and invariably brought them all to their feet, a reaction an actor rarely achieves in a long career. The front row into which I was hurled often produced reactions most actors never see. Old ladies wielding handbags yelled abuse at Charles and pin-stripe-suited stockbroker types bemoaned the fact that, now the leading actor had killed himself, their ticket money and evening out were lost. I am sorry for all the shopping bags and picnic boxes I smashed as I crashed to the feet of the front row, but it was good theatre, and I never met a member of any audience that didn't think it had happened only on their night.

It was this particular move that caused the only serious accident during the run at Stratford. In a performance just before Christmas I had a bad fall. I was on my way into the front row and I landed right on the point of my right shoulder, separating my acromio-clavicular joint. I love the sound of that part of my anatomy, verbal, not actual. I slumped to the floor at the feet of the front row, and lay there grimacing. Occasionally a member of the audience would help me back on to the stage, but not this time. I assumed I had broken something in my shoulder, and decided the best thing to do was to stay there. Charles, my opponent, had other ideas. To my utter horror Terry Wood appeared over the edge of the stage and bent down to help me up. In the true spirit of the theatre yours truly scrambled to his feet and managed one more desperate flying drop-kick before Duke

Frederick, appreciating the agony I was in, mercifully came out with the words, 'No more, no more.' But there was more. Having scraped through the rest of the scene, I left the stage to be greeted by the Company Manager, Nick Jones, who had miraculously found a doctor in what seemed like seconds. If I thought the pain I was already suffering was bad, this doctor was about to prove me wrong. Out of earshot of the audience and the other actors a needle the size of a knitting needle was plunged into my shoulder and waggled about until it found the appropriate cavity, where it delivered its painkiller. The relief was instantaneous, and although it began to wear off after an hour or so, it got me through the show. But I shall never forget that needle, and Nick Jones will never forget the agony it caused me. So I was out of the show for a couple of months.

John Bowe, 'Orlando',
Players of Shakespeare, ed. Philip Brockbank,
1985, pp. 70–1.

Peter Ustinov plays King Lear at Stratford, Ontario, in 1979.

We can always do with a few more laughs, and Ustinov gives us a lot we need: 'I've got three daughters, which is a more thorough rehearsal for the part than anything Stanislavsky ever suggested.'

Maurice Good,
Every Inch a Lear: A Rehearsal Journal,
1982, p. 224.

Sinead Cusack

Actress, 1949–

As You Like It at Stratford-upon-Avon, 1982.

When Terry Hands was directing *As You* he showed us all the costume designs, which we admired. And when I looked at mine for Arden I said, 'Terry, my costume as Celia is *green.*' 'Yes,' he said. 'You haven't got a superstition about wearing green on stage, have you?' 'No, no!' 'You're Irish, aren't you?'

I said, 'Of course I'm Irish. I'm not superstitious about the colour. It's just that I'm green and so is the set. If I'm green and the set's green, I'm going to disappear into the set.' And he said, 'Don't be so stupid, Sinead. You *are* the set.'

As a result of that little exchange, I became a very obvious and determined and available Celia. I sat centre stage.

Sinead Cusack,
Clamorous Voices, Carol Rutter, 1988, p. 115.

Antony Sher

Actor, writer, 1949–

Richard III at the Barbican, 1985.

Monday 21 November

A DAY AT THE BARBICAN

. . . At the top of the main staircase there is a plaque unveiled by the Queen at the Gala Opening on 3 March 1982. I was present and had an encounter which now seems to have a curious significance.

I was leading a little group to this staircase for the arrival of the Queen. Apart from Jim, the group consisted of RSC stalwarts Adrian Noble and Joyce Nettles. They knew the building much better than I did, as I hadn't even joined the company, so why I should have been leading is something of a mystery. At the time I put it down to drunkenness – champagne had been flowing freely – but now I suspect it was more to do with a Greater Scheme Of Things. Anyway, leading I was. The Royal arrival was imminent. DJs and evening gowns shimmered and rustled; the lights tickled over jewellery and hair lacquer; the smell of exclusive scents, the sounds of sophisticated gossip and discreet champagne burps.

I turned back to beckon my flagging group and almost immediately crashed into someone heading in the other direction. I say crashed, but it was as soft and cushioned as befits a collision with Destiny. The recipient of my careless shoulder was an old man with a white beard and rimless spectacles. The face was vaguely familiar, the voice even more so.

'Are you trying to kill me?' he asked with the gentle humour of someone who has looked Death properly in the eye.

'No,' I replied with certainty. And then as an afterthought, 'Sorry.'

And that's all there was to it. That's all that was said. It was puzzling that a little circle had cleared around us, me and Father Time, but not unduly worrying. He smiled and passed on. I joined my group who now stared at me with an assortment of strange expressions, as if they had witnessed some miracle. I smiled, nonplussed, a little drunk, and made to lead on.

'Do you know who that was?' demanded Jim.

The urgency of his voice caused me to swing round and stare after the retreating figure. Suddenly I recognised him, or rather recognised his wife – she was holding his arm now and steering him, to avoid further collisions with drunken actors in hired DJs – Joan Plowright.

The Queen arrived, but my encounter had so stunned me that I was pointing in the wrong direction, expecting her to come down the stairs instead of up them, and missed seeing her altogether.

It didn't matter, for I had just brushed shoulders with Richard III.

Antony Sher, *Year of the King*, 1985, pp. 30–1.

•

The logistics of managing a show into production and managing it whilst in the repertoire is not a subject which appears to command much directorial time . . . To take one instance of this, I have seen the fascinating problems for the stage crew of coping with several productions in the theatre at once. The embarrassingly late curtain-up on 18 June [1983] was due to the crew's difficulty in handling for the first time a changeover from a matinée of *Twelfth Night* (which has a pretty but elaborate and cumbersome set) to an evening performance of *Julius Caesar* (which has many pieces in its sets, including a large wagon), following the addition to the repertoire of *Henry VIII* (which has an overhead railway from which some 30 large silhouettes are hung). This railway must be taken down to make way for other productions. It, and every other set not in use, has to be stored in the theatre to be out of the way of succeeding productions and yet readily accessible when it is next required.

Financial Scrutiny of the Royal Shakespeare Company, Vols I and II.
Report to the Earl of Gowrie, Minister for the Arts, by Clive Priestley, C.B.
London: HMSO, 1984, p. 204.

Ron Daniels's production of *Julius Caesar* . . . opened at Stratford in March 1983. A noisy piece of braggadocio, it offered spectacular gimmicks as a substitute for clear ideas about the play. Its search for such ideas, however, led it to make an unexpected contribution to a general election campaign. Four MPs and three journalists were invited to pronounce, in the programme, on whether or not the conspirators were right to assassinate Caesar. Michael Foot, then Leader of the Labour Party, said that they were and a month later, with an election imminent, found himself under attack on the features page of *The Times* for his irresponsible views on political murder.

Nicholas Shrimpton,
'Shakespeare Performances in Stratford-upon-Avon and London, 1982–3',
Shakespeare Survey 37, 1984, p. 172.

Kenneth Branagh

Actor-manager, writer, 1960–

Kenneth Branagh prepares for *Henry V* at Stratford-upon-Avon, 1984.

But it was much more difficult to get my imagination around Henry's royal status, the isolation of his role as spiritual and military leader. Quite simply, what was it *like* being a king? As with war there was plenty of written material, but there was no one to talk to, no one with whom I could exchange ideas. In a welter of indulgent frustration I would bore my friends at the numerous suppers that accompanied my last weeks in London before the move to Stratford. Very early one morning, after a spectacularly verbose evening, my dinner party host rang me to say that he felt something might be done about my problem.

A week later I was motoring up the long gravel drive to Kensington Palace. After a week of meetings, I had been vetted and through several contacts I had been given an introduction to the Prince of Wales. Getting the afternoon off rehearsal had been rather tricky, but I decided to abandon the notion of toothache and come clean with Adrian [Noble]. A director of the *Royal* Shakespeare Company could hardly refuse such a request, and I swore him to secrecy. The heir to the throne did not wish to be plagued by the membership of Equity, all requesting advice on regal roles. I felt several bonds of allegiance: firstly to the chum who had helped organise it, to his friend, and, of course, to the Prince himself, who I felt must be fed up with continual minor betrayals.

My grubby green car came to a halt by the security hut, and the policeman waved me through. My God, they really did expect me. I walked to the front door without being ambushed by three hundred security guards and when the door opened the footman greeted me with, 'Mr Branagh?'

I waited downstairs in a room filled with Royal Wedding memorabilia. The footman who brought me a cup of tea explained that the trays, pictures and mugs were all gifts sent by members of the public, and that this was one way of using them. I wondered with alarm what exactly I was going to ask the heir to the throne, but the time for panicking was over, and I was shown upstairs and into the Prince's drawing-room where he shook my hand warmly, smiled and said, 'I really have no idea how I can help you, but please sit down, and let's have a chat.'

I felt an instant rapport. I had never encountered such an extraordinary and genuine humility. It would be all right.

'Well, sir, I know it seems rather strange. I'm not intending my Henry V to be an impersonation of you, but I simply wanted to explain some of my feelings about the character, particularly his role as king. They're not necessarily highly academic or intellectual observations, but as you're in a unique position to comment, I'd love to run them past you, and if you have anything to say about them I'd be most grateful. You don't *have* to say anything.'

I began Henry's spiritual checklist. It seemed to me that royalty involved the suppression of many facets of one's character. In Henry this meant (as has been proven by many productions) that the sense of humour which I felt belonged to the man was often missing, as was his latent violence, in fact all the normal extremes of human behaviour which in ordinary mortals find their own balance but which in a pressurised monarch could emerge with even greater force. I wanted my Henry to display these unexpected qualities with tremendous intensity, and I felt that Shakespeare's text encouraged this view. Prince Charles concurred: yes, there was a tremendous pressure and temptation to be at times either very silly or very violent. As with most people, these impulses were resisted but the underlying pressure was greater than most people would ever experience.

Henry's isolation was another fascinating area. Through the course of the play a number of betrayals take place: his 'bed-fellow,' Lord Scroop, is discovered leading an assassination attempt; his former mentor, Falstaff, dies; and later still he is required to order the execution of another former drinking companion, Bardolph. His loneliness is intense and his hurt at the various betrayals and losses is very acute. I asked Prince Charles whether the various newspaper betrayals of events, dramatic and mundane, had changed him. Yes, it had, profoundly. And it had, as I suspected was true of Henry, produced an extraordinary melancholy. It was a sadness that could either produce bitterness or a more useful but painful wisdom, and Prince Charles had clearly developed the latter. He bore the inevitable bruises of his position with great courage, and although, sitting opposite him, I could detect the haunted look of responsibility, the very fact that he was speaking to me was an indication of his continuing desire to give people the benefit of the doubt.

Loneliness, however, was unavoidable. Henry makes one desperate attempt in the play to be like other men. During the famous night-time sequence, he walks among his men in disguise. The experience is extremely unsatisfactory: he wants to be one of them, but he can't be; he wants them to understand his position but they resist it. Had Prince Charles ever felt like doing the same? Yes, while he was at Cambridge he'd attempted to do the same thing, but the results were disastrous. By the end of the night-time sequence in *Henry V*, the young king's only comfort is the very certainty of his lifelong isolation. The young Hal had at least the taste of the Boar's Head life, but when he became king there could be no such contact with an ordinary existence.

There is little solace to be found in such remoteness. I believed that Henry's only real comfort could be his faith, and Prince Charles was in total agreement. Some kind of belief in God was the only practical way of living from day to day, it was the only way to deal with his position. This confirmed what I felt I should try to convey in Henry. I didn't wish to present Henry as a tortured martyr, but I did feel strongly that a complex psychological portrait had been set up by Shakespeare which included guilt, doubt and self-questioning. Prince Charles's comments were immensely helpful and I had the impression that he shared with Shakespeare's Henry a desire to strike a delicate balance between responsibility and compassion.

Kenneth Branagh, *Beginning*, 1989, pp. 141–4.

Declan Donnellan

Director, 1953–

Declan Donnellan, director of the Cheek By Jowl company, responds to an interview provocation in support of Malvolio.

Interviewer May I raise my voice in favour of the fellow who just likes to get some sleep in during the small hours and would prefer the noisy party to go somewhere else?

Declan Donnellan I know, I know. We just had a lady in Sicily (where the company was playing *The Tempest*) who did exactly that to us. We'd just opened the show there and we were having a drink on the terrace in the hotel. It was very late, and this English lady stormed out and made this wonderful speech. It was pure kitchen scene. 'You have made me ashamed to be British.' And we'd only been talking, we hadn't been actually carousing and singing 'Tilly-vally, Lady!' The second thing was, 'I have heard from the hotel people that you are theatricals. If so, so much the worse for you!' It was very salutary for us. Now I know what it's like to be the sort of English person that people are ashamed of abroad. She was silhouetted in the moonlight, too, it was as in a romantic production of *Twelfth Night*. She almost came on with a gold chain round her shoulders.

Ralph Berry,
On Directing Shakespeare: Interviews with contemporary directors, 1989, pp. 195–6.

•

Hamlet at the National Theatre, 1989, was sponsored by Ladbrokes.

I suppose there's something appropriate about Ladbrokes sponsoring a production of *Hamlet*. The duel between Hamlet and Laertes is the only one in Shakespeare that is fought for a bet and I detected a definite stir of interest in the somnolent Ladbroke executive beside me when Hamlet assured Horatio that he would 'win at the odds'.

. . . When Polonius commissions Reynaldo in convoluted fashion to spy on his son he actually loses the thread of his argument: 'And then, sir, does 'a this –'a does – what was I about to say? By the mass, I was about to say something. Where did I leave?' Reynaldo jogs his memory: 'At "closes in the consequence," ay, marry.' As played by Michael Bryant, it was a wonderful theatrical joke that had the audience half wondering whether the actor had forgotten his lines.

For some people, more than half. On the way out I met a theatre critic of a national newspaper whose only comment on the evening was to express astonishment at this lapse from an actor of Michael Bryant's experience: 'Still, he covered it up pretty well.'

Sean French, 'Diary', *New Statesman and Nation*,
23 March 1989.

A racist outburst in Stratford has shocked actors of the Royal Shakespeare Company, while indicating that acceptance of mixed-race casting is not yet universal. The incident happened on July 27, minutes into a performance of *King Lear*, and was triggered by the entrance of the black actor, Clarence Smith, who was playing the King of France. At first, an indistinct mutter was heard from the circle. Then, as Smith delivered the line 'This is most strange,' referring to Lear's capricious treatment of Cordelia, a woman was heard to proclaim 'It most certainly is.'

The woman then held forth during the interval. 'It is an insult to La France to cast a black actor as king,' she announced, in a French accent, promising further protests should the actor reappear on stage. (He did not.) The fact that a white English actor would be no more French than a black one did not seem to have occurred to her. Later, Sally Dexter, the actress playing Regan, said she had 'never been so shocked in my whole life.'

The Times, 'Briefing', 9 August 1990.

Out out brief candle, indeed. Keeping the flame alight during the famous Lady Macbeth scene in the Open Air Theatre's production in Regent's Park was never going to be easy in such a summer. Then Nicola McAuliffe, who plays the part, decided she would prefer to plunge her hands not into a candle, but into a bowl of fire.

The Magician's Circle was consulted and suggested an illusion created with a borax solution. But the actress wanted the real thing. 'Richard van Allen, the opera singer, said he had seen a fire-resistant gel on *Tomorrow's World*, which if coated on the flesh would resist temperatures of up to 600° C.'

The BBC put her in contact with the manufacturers, who said there was just one difficulty: the gel is green. Following requests from stunt men and circus acts they had manufactured about 2 lb in a flesh colour, but the last of this went to

Pinewood for *Aliens 3*. 'I asked if the studio had any spare, and they gave me enough for my scene,' says McAuliffe.

How is the production faring in the face of the adverse elements? 'We have had lots of Japanese tourists, who sit without coats or umbrellas, getting soaked. They love it. They think this is what British culture is all about.'

'Diary', *The Times*, 26 June 1991.

Ian Charleson

Actor, 1950–1990

Ian Charleson played a memorable Hamlet at the Royal National Theatre, while in the final stages of AIDS. His first performance was on 9 October 1989, and the last on 13 November 1989. After that last performance, Ian McKellen records:

In the green room afterwards, he was overwhelmed with praise and exceptional enthusiasm. He was hugging a bottle of champagne from an admiring theatre critic. Only when he got safely home did he give in to exhaustion. He didn't work again. But he knew he'd been remarkably good and during his last eight weeks often talked about *Hamlet*, with a paperback script of it by his bed.

For Ian Charleson: A Tribute, 1990, pp. 129–30.

Index

For Product Safety Concerns and Information please contact our EU representative GPSR@taylorandfrancis.com
Taylor & Francis Verlag GmbH, Kaufingerstraße 24, 80331 München, Germany

www.ingramcontent.com/pod-product-compliance
Lightning Source LLC
LaVergne TN
LVHW010600110826
845149LV00003B/712
9781138659599